SPEAK TO THE MOUNTAINS!

*Prayers & Prophetic Decrees For
The 7 Mountains of Cultural Influence*

COPYRIGHT © 2018 – I.R. WOMACK
SPEAK TO THE MOUNTAINS!
All Rights Reserved

All Scripture quotations, unless otherwise indicated, are taken from the New King James Version®. Copyright © 1982 by Thomas Nelson. Used by permission. All rights reserved.

Scripture quotations marked (AMP) are taken from the Amplified Bible, Copyright © 1954, 1958, 1962, 1964, 1965, 1987 by The Lockman Foundation. Used by permission.

Scripture quotations marked (NLT) are taken from the Holy Bible, New Living Translation, copyright ©1996, 2004, 2007, 2013, 2015 by Tyndale House Foundation. Used by permission of Tyndale House Publishers, Inc., Carol Stream, Illinois 60188. All rights reserved.

Scripture quotations marked (NIV) are taken from the Holy Bible, New International Version®, NIV®. Copyright © 1973, 1978, 1984, 2011 by Biblica, Inc.™ Used by permission of Zondervan. All rights reserved worldwide. www.zondervan.com The "NIV" and "New International Version" are trademarks registered in the United States Patent and Trademark Office by Biblica, Inc.™

INTRO, 7 MOUNTAIN SUMMARIES, DON'T GET LEFT BEHIND - COPYRIGHT © 2017 Axel Sippach All Rights Reserved – Used by permission
CULTIVATING IDENTITY AND PURPOSE IN OUR CHILDREN - COPYRIGHT © 2017 Tony & Nicole Davis All Rights Reserved – Used by permission
GENERATIONAL BONDAGE AND CURSES - COPYRIGHT © 2017 Anita Etta - All Rights Reserved – Used by permission
ERADICATING THE SPIRIT OF POVERTY IN OUR FAMILIES - COPYRIGHT © 2017 Sarafia Jones-Hall - All Rights Reserved – Used by permission
PROTECTING OUR CHILDREN - COPYRIGHT © 2017 Olympia Jarboe - All Rights Reserved – Used by permission
THE RESTORATION OF THE FAMILY UNIT - COPYRIGHT © 2017 Christine Cline - All Rights Reserved – Used by permission
MARRIAGE AND FAMILY - COPYRIGHT © 2017 Noreen N. Henry - All Rights Reserved – Used by permission
SEEDS OF EDEN - COPYRIGHT © 2017 Cynthia Williams-Bey - All Rights Reserved – Used by permission
EXPOSING DARK POWERS & RELEASING TRUE LIGHT! - A 7 MOUNTAIN FORECAST - COPYRIGHT © 2017 - Yolanda L. Powell - All Rights Reserved – Used by permission
GLOBAL MEDIA - COPYRIGHT © 2017 Cherie Banks - All Rights Reserved – Used by permission
WHO IS SHAPING WHO? - COPYRIGHT © 2017 Alexander Gray - All Rights Reserved – Used by permission
SCHOOL-TO-PRISON PIPELINE - COPYRIGHT © 2017 Donita Gordon, Ed. S - All Rights Reserved – Used by permission
SEPARATION OF CHURCH AND STATE - COPYRIGHT © 2017 Tressena Jones - All Rights Reserved – Used by permission

DECODING THE HEALTH CRISES - COPYRIGHT © 2017 Shelby Frederick - All Rights Reserved – Used by permission

JUSTICE ON THE MOUNTAIN OF EDUCATION - COPYRIGHT © 2017 Joy Witter – All Rights Reserved – Used by permission

THE INTENT AND PURPOSE OF THE ARTS - COPYRIGHT © 2017 Niles Bess - All Rights Reserved – Used by permission

SUBLIMINAL MESSAGES ON THE MOUNTAIN OF ENTERTAINMENT - COPYRIGHT © 2017 Michelle Jackson - All Rights Reserved – Used by permission

A PROPHETIC VOICE ON THE MOUNTAIN OF ARTS & ENTERTAINMENT - COPYRIGHT © 2017 Dr. James Pinto - All Rights Reserved – Used by permission

THE EAGLE ANOINTING - COPYRIGHT © 2017 - LaDonna Jackson - All Rights Reserved – Used by permission

DEMONSTRATING A LIVING CHURCH IN A DYING CULTURE - COPYRIGHT © 2017 - Anita McCoy - All Rights Reserved – Used by permission

WHERE ARE MY PRIESTS? - COPYRIGHT © 2017 Adrienne Sumler - All Rights Reserved – Used by permission

INFLUENCE OF THE NEW AGE MOVEMENT IN THE CHURCH - COPYRIGHT © 2017 Roseline Keni - All Rights Reserved – Used by permission

SOUNDING THE TRUMPET OF AWAKENING IN THE NEW SEASON OF REVIVAL - COPYRIGHT © 2017 Thapelo Kgabage - All Rights Reserved – Used by permission

SPIRITUAL SONSHIP COPYRIGHT © 2017 Alandis Porter - All Rights Reserved – Used by permission

THE TIME TO START YOUR BUSINESS—IS NOW! COPYRIGHT © 2017 Yolanda Mosby - All Rights Reserved – Used by permission

WEALTH CREATION FOR KINGDOM ADVANCEMENT COPYRIGHT © 2017 Amanda Samuels - All Rights Reserved – Used by permission

THE SUPERNATURAL DIMENSION OF THE APOSTOLIC ENTREPRENEUR COPYRIGHT © 2017 Jonelle Maxwell - All Rights Reserved – Used by permission

INFLUENCE ON THE BUSINESS MOUNTAIN COPYRIGHT © 2017 Carla Wallace - All Rights Reserved – Used by permission

ECONOMICS FOR THE GOOD SEED COPYRIGHT © 2017 Shevon L. Sampson - All Rights Reserved – Used by permission

UNITED NATIONS COPYRIGHT © 2017 Michelle Brown - All Rights Reserved – Used by permission

KINGDOM STRATEGIES FOR THE MOUNTAIN OF GOVERNMENT COPYRIGHT © 2017 Kenna O'Flannigan - All Rights Reserved – Used by permission

THE WILLIE LYNCH CURSE COPYRIGHT © 2017 Jackie Betty - All Rights Reserved – Used by permission

ISBN: 978-0-9997159-3-2

TABLE OF CONTENTS

Introduction 1

CHAPTER 1: The Mountain of Family 10
    Parenting: Cultivating Identity and Purpose in Our Children 11
    Generational Bondage and Curses 18
    Eradicating The Spirit of Poverty in Our Families 24
    Protecting Our Children 29
    The Restoration of the Family Unit 34
    Marriage and Family 40
    Seeds of Eden 45

CHAPTER 2: The Mountain Of Media 50
    Exposing Dark Powers & Releasing True Light! 51
    Don't Get Left Behind 56
    Global Media: Influencing Today's Culture and Fulfilling Biblical Prophecy 65
    Who is Shaping Who? How Media Influences the Masses 71

CHAPTER 3: The Mountain of Education 77
    School-To-Prison Pipeline 79
    Separation of Church and State: Bridging the Gap 83
    Decoding the Health Crises 88
    Justice on the Mountain of Education 93

CHAPTER 4: The Mountain of Arts & Entertainment 98
    The Intent and Purpose of the Arts 100
    Subliminal Messages on the Mountain of Entertainment 104
    A Prophetic Voice on the Mountain of Arts & Entertainment 108

CHAPTER 5: The Mountain of Religion 113

    The Eagle Anointing: Mantled to Destroy Oppression in Cults 115

    Demonstrating a Living Church in a Dying Culture 121

    Where are My Priests? 127

    Influence of the New Age Movement in the Church 134

    Sounding the Trumpet of Awakening in the New Season of Revival 141

    Spiritual Sonship 145

CHAPTER 6: The Mountain of Business 150

    The Time to Start Your Business—Is Now! 151

    Wealth Creation for Kingdom Advancement 155

    The Supernatural Dimension of the Apostolic Entrepreneur 160

    Influence on the Business Mountain 166

    Economics for the Good Seed 170

CHAPTER 7: The Mountain of Government 175

    United Nations: A Gateway Into Global Reformation 176

    Kingdom Strategies for the Mountain of Government 183

    The Willie Lynch Curse: A Spiritual Battle We Must Win! 188

CHAPTER 8: A 7 Mountain Forecast: Where Do We Go From Here? 194

    Meet The Co-Authors 204

INTRODUCTION

The dawning of a new day is upon the Church. 2017 marked the 500th anniversary of the momentous Protestant Reformation that forever changed the spiritual landscape of Europe, bringing much of the continent out of 1000 years of spiritual dark ages into the light of a new day. It was not just a new season—it was a new era of major apostolic disruption that erupted on the scene through the pioneering efforts of Martin Luther and others. Millions came out of darkness into the light of truth in that generation. Since that time, the past 500 years in the Church have been seasons of revival, reformation, and restoration, as God has been revealing more and more present truth from Scripture, creating more transformation in and through the Church.

A New Era

And now, a new day is upon us again, with a new era of apostolic reformation no longer looming on the distant horizon. A major focus of this fresh, disruptive movement is being referred to as the *7 Mountain Mandate*—perhaps one of the most radical and transformative reformation movements we have seen, with the potential to see powerful advances of God's Kingdom on the Earth in this generation and beyond.

This book, *Speak to the Mountains*, will be covering these seven mountains of culture that influence society and nations and inspire you to be a part of this powerful Kingdom movement. More on this later, but let me briefly introduce myself.

Apostle to the Nations

For more than three decades now, it has been my incredible honor to represent the Lord Jesus Christ, as He has called and sent me as an apostle to more than 90 countries, preaching and teaching the Word of God and things pertaining to his Kingdom. I have traveled more than nine million miles around the world, discipling the nations and raising up spiritual sons and daughters. It truly has been an exciting journey and tremendous apostolic adventure that has shaped my life and ministry, transforming me into the apostle I have become today.

In the 1980's and 90's, much of my apostleship was focused on Muslim and Communist nations where the Church was being severely persecuted, strengthening the believers, which also included smuggling thousands of Bibles and spiritual books to them. Later, my apostolic ministry expanded into other parts of the world where there was a great hunger for present biblical truth, the apostolic, the prophetic, and revival.

Over the past 20 years, I have been involved with what has been coined the New Apostolic Reformation movement (NAR), seeing God do amazing things in the nations. At an age now where most people are retiring, the Lord has given me the mandate to pioneer a new apostolic network called the EPIC Global Network. E.P.I.C. is an acronym for Extraordinary People Influencing Culture. The four pillars of EPIC are the apostolic, the prophetic, revival/evangelism, and the 7 Mountain Mandate. EPIC was launched in August 2015 and is seeing great momentum and growth. I see our tribe as an Apostolic 2.0—next-generation apostolic movement, and something I am committed to giving the rest of my life to.

What is the 7 Mountain Mandate?

Many people, upon hearing this term for the first time, are asking the question: What is the 7 Mountain Mandate? Scripture is replete with references concerning mountains in both the New and Old Testaments. Certain mountains were places of encounter where God met with those He had chosen, such as Moses and Mt. Sinai and Jesus and the Mt. of Transfiguration.

Mountains were also places of confrontation between light and darkness, such as Mt. Carmel where the Prophet Elijah confronts backslidden Israel and challenges the 450 prophets of Baal and 400 false prophets of Asherah to a contest. Mt. Zion, a high point in Jerusalem, was where King David ruled after taking the stronghold from the Jebusites and established his palace and the Tabernacle of David there. The heavenly cosmic mountain called Mt. Zion is the spiritual counterpart of it. It is the place where God dwells and from where He rules and reigns, and is now the place where believers dwell with Him (Hebrews 12:22-24).

The biblical theology of mountains is incredibly important for us to understand God's greater Kingdom plan and purpose. It becomes a hermeneutical lens that helps us see the spiritual dynamics taking place in the invisible realm more clearly in Scripture. It also helps in framing a biblical worldview for us that inspires and motivates us to pursue our destiny and calling in Christ more passionately.

The 7 Mountain Mandate has its modern-day inception with two great apostolic giants of the faith who have pioneered some of the largest youth movements in the world: Loren Cunningham, founder of Youth with a Mission (YWAM), and Bill Bright, founder of Campus Crusade for Christ. In August of 1975, these two leaders had lunch and were comparing notes of what God was speaking to them. Surprisingly, they both on the same day received the same revelation from the Lord concerning the seven spheres of influence that are the mind-molders of society, culture, and nations. They began to share it with their movements, but it did not gain much global traction in that season.

A few years ago, some current apostolic leaders from the New Apostolic Reformation movement (about 20+ years old now) picked up that revelation and began to develop it more in the framework of using the term *mountains* rather than just *spheres*. The message began to gain traction and is becoming an apostolic mandate for our generation.

Briefly, the seven mountains are: Mountain of Religion; Mountain of Family; Mountain of Government; Mountain of Business; Mountain of Arts and Entertainment; Mountain of Media; and Mountain of Education. Of course, there are many hills or subcategories such as Sports which could be under the Mountain of Arts and Entertainment, and Science and

Technology which could be under the Business Mountain, etc. But these seven mountains are the primary mind-molders of culture that influence cities and nations, and the 3-8% that reach the tops of these mountains are the dominant influencers of the whole mountain.

Foundational 7 Mountain Mandate Scriptures

Isaiah 2: 1-5 and Micah 4:1-7 speak of the mountain of the Lord's temple (palace, house, court) being established as chief or highest among the mountains; or you could say ruler of the mountains. And as this happens, all nations/all peoples will flow or "stream" up to it. It's interesting that in Jeremiah 51:44, God is pronouncing judgment on Bel, the dark fallen prince who ruled in Babylon, and God says He will make Bel spew out what he has swallowed, and that the nations will no longer "stream" to Bel because the wall of Babylon had fallen. The Hebrew for "stream" is "Nahar" and is the same as in Isaiah 2:2. So we see a reversal taking place; whereas the nations had streamed to satanic fallen princes and were swallowed up, so to speak, by them, and they now would stream to the Mountain of the Lord as the rulership of overcoming believers, who understand they are kings, is exercised on the tops of the seven mountains.

Do you see it? Do you see the picture here? Jesus is building His Church—His *ekklesia* at the very gates of hell and they cannot prevail. He has given us the key of the Kingdom to bind and loose and to transact Kingdom business on the Earth. And God is raising a company of sons and daughters—Daniel, Joseph, and Esther overcomers who will rule and reign with Christ as "kings and priests" on the tops of the mountains so that the nations will flow up to the house of the Lord.

Obadiah verse 21 speaks of "deliverers" going up on Mt. Zion to govern the mountains of Esau, and that the kingdom of Esau will be the Lord's. God is calling His sons and daughters to begin to take their rightful place with Christ and learn how to rule and reign on the mountains. So, the 7 Mountain Mandate becomes an incredible template for spiritual warfare. It was the missing piece needed to begin to see greater healing, restoration, and transformation of cities and nations.

This is where we are headed—not just ministry in the church, but ministry in the marketplace; not just Sunday in the church facility being sacred space, but seeing your work as a sacred space. Why? Because everywhere you go is sacred space. It's called marketplace ministry!

Everywhere the soles of your feet touch is sacred space because the Spirit of God is in you and because you are the temple of the Holy Spirit. Isaiah 52:7 in the NIV says: *"How beautiful on the mountains are the feet of those who bring good news, who proclaim peace, who bring good tidings, who proclaim salvation, who say to Zion, 'Your God reigns!'"* Your feet are beautiful and anointed to go!

In Babylon—Not of Babylon

The 7 Mountain message and mandate is about being salt and light influencers—a city set upon a hill whose light cannot be hidden. You are called to be Daniels in Babylon, Josephs in Egypt, and Esthers in Persia. You are *in* Babylon but not *of* Babylon, and Bel will give and is giving up the harvest because God has judged him.

And we are the authorized, Holy Spirit-energized, and empowered judicial witnesses, called upon to carry out the sentence on the mountain tops through our gifts, talents, abilities, calling, and destiny. Are you up to the task—to the calling? May we learn more and more to reign in this life as kings and realize that we are the vice-regents of the King of kings and Lord of lords, even Jesus Christ, who is now ruling and reigning on the eternal throne of David in Heaven at the right hand of the Majesty on High!

Kings and Priests

The Bible calls us "kings and priests." And we are kings and priests after the ancient Order of Melchizedek—the Order of which Jesus has been made our faithful High Priest. We are the Bene Yitzhar, which is the Hebrew term for "Sons of Fresh Oil"— the ones who stand beside the Lord of all the Earth to serve him as revealed in Zechariah 4.

We are sons of God that Jesus has brought to Heaven through the new birth experience to enter into a divine partnership with Heaven, to reclaim the Earth for the King. Sons of God are who we are—it's our identity in Christ. Kings and priests are our job descriptions. The nations are Christ's inheritance, and we are in partnership with Heaven to reclaim the Earth. These seven mountains represent the kingdoms or systems of this world we need to focus our attention on. And God has given us a blueprint for dominion and conquest.

Speak To This Mountain! What Mountain Was Jesus Referring To?

When you try to understand Scripture in context, and travel back in history and put yourself in first-century Israel, the Word of God can unfold in a whole new and fresh way, and you begin to see things you never saw before. In Matthew 17: 20-21, Jesus said that if you have *"faith like a mustard seed, you can say to this mountain, Move from here to there and it will move. Nothing is impossible for you."* He repeats it in Matthew 21:21, that if we have faith and do not doubt, just as the fig tree withered when Jesus spoke to it, so also must this mountain obey and be thrown into the sea when we speak to it.

Is it possible that "this mountain" He was speaking of was the Herodian? The Herodian was a huge 18-story-high, man-made mountain the wealthy, wicked, and hedonistic ruler King Herod the Great ("king of the Jews") constructed on 44 acres near Bethlehem on the highest hill in Judean desert, which took over 15 years to build. The Herodian could be seen from many miles away.

But the true King of the Jews and King of all Creation says, "Hey, you think that's such a big deal? If you have faith as a mustard seed, you can tell that mountain, that represents the demonic kingdom of a demonized tyrant, be removed and cast into the sea." Wow! That makes this Scripture take on a whole lot more meaning. It's about the kingdoms of this world becoming the Kingdom of our God and Christ—King Jesus! It's about the kind of faith and prayer that can move demonically-inspired man-made mountains that resist the Kingdom of God out of the way to make room for the Kingdom of God.

This is the same Herod the Great that was looking to kill Jesus when He was born and killed all the babies near Bethlehem that were two years old and under. When he died, Jesus and His family came back from Egypt. Herod's son, Herod Antipas, was the one who later beheaded John the Baptist. He had his father's DNA. In Acts chapter 4, the believers prayed for God to deal with Herod's threats. In Acts 12, God answered by sending an angel to strike Herod down while he was giving a speech in his royal robes on his royal throne. Then he got eaten up by worms—not a very *royal* way to go.

I believe "this mountain" Jesus was referring to was The Herodian—Herod the Great's man-made mountain; the project of the same Herod who tried to kill the baby Jesus.

But the Greatest King, the true King of the Jews says this mountain of Herod, by mustard seed-faith, can be thrown into the sea. All you have to do is speak to the mountain, and it must obey you.

As sons and daughters of God, we have a heavenly mandate, a high calling to see His Kingdom and will be done on the Earth as in Heaven. We are the anointed *sons of fresh oil* who are "kings and priests" after the ancient Order of Melchizedek, on a mission to disciple nations, heal the nations, reclaim the Earth, and bring Heaven on Earth to rule and reign with Him. It is part of the high calling of God in Christ Jesus we must press into.

Speak To the Mountains Anthology

Speak to the Mountains!, the book you have picked up and are looking through, is an anthology with over 30 writers contributing a sub-chapter each, covering a certain aspect of one of the seven mountains of influence. I believe this anthology will open your eyes to begin to see that God is calling you beyond just *going* to church, to actually *being* the Church: the ekklesia that Jesus said He is building right at the very "gates of hell" (the open doors of satanic influence on these seven mountains of influence that affect our cities and nations).

Nimrod, the founder of Babylon, in Genesis 11 leads an outright satanic rebellion, conspiring against Yahweh by motivating and mobilizing the people to build the Tower of Babel and a city reaching into the Heavens in the plain of Shinar (modern-day Iraq). I believe he thought this was the location of the former Garden of Eden and was employing the use of dark occult arts to find and reopen the portal to Heaven that was once opened in the Garden. Yahweh would have none of it, so He came down and confused their unified language and totally wrecked their current plan. "Babel" in Hebrew means "gate of god" or "gate of the gods" before it came to mean "confusion."

These seven mountains of influence are man-made kingdoms and systems like Babylon that are now under the control of fallen satanic dark lords. They are like The Herodian—that man-made mountain Jesus said we have authority to speak to and cast into the sea. The demonic powers ruling the tops of these mountains must and will yield to the power of the anointed sons of God; kings and priests after the order of Melchizedek, who are developing the mustard faith to speak and cast them into the sea.

Speaking to mountains is your birthright as sons of God. The mountain of the Lord's temple—Zion—the Kingdom Mountain, will rule over these mountains. The kingdoms of this world shall become the Kingdom of our Lord and of His Christ, and He will reign forever and ever. The gospel of the Kingdom is good news. And it is glorious. It will accomplish all that the New Covenant has secured. There is no defeat. A world without end—glory in the Church!

In Speak to the Mountains, you will find information and revelation, along with inspiration and motivation to discover and pursue your mission and assignments on one or more of the seven mountains of influence. Some of you are called to Ephesians' five-fold ministry in the Church. That may only be 10% or less. But for the other 90%, your ministry is marketplace ministry on one or more of these mountains. As you read this anthology, get ready for your eyes to be opened as you embark on an exciting journey of discovery that I believe will lead to a fresh pursuit of destiny and purpose.

The mountains await your beautiful feet, and the good news you carry to them! Go into all the world. Proclaim the good news. Let your light shine!

Axel Sippach

CHAPTER 1

THE MOUNTAIN OF FAMILY

Family is the foundation—the building block of all society. God established the concept of *family* before any other mountain concept: one man + one woman = family (Genesis 2:23,24; Matthew 19:4-6). The Mountain of Family is being usurped by satanic forces in America and many other nations, as chaos has been unleashed against it to attempt to redefine the fundamental definition of marriage. When the family breaks down, it opens the door for all kinds of social problems to follow. The Church which in 1 Timothy 3:15 states is the "pillar and foundation of truth" must rise up to reclaim this mountain and stand up for the institution of marriage and family.

The blessing or curse of God is passed down to future generations through this mountain, bringing us to the area of fatherlessness that must also be addressed, as it is epidemic in many nations and destroying many lives. Malachi 4:6 speaks of Elijah coming to turn the hearts of the fathers to the children, and the hearts of the children to the fathers. Jesus said John the Baptist was the Elijah to come. But I believe that the spirit, mantle, and anointing of Elijah are still available for us to walk in today, having one of the primary powerful results of turning hearts – especially the heart of the fathers first to the sons and daughters. I believe this is a key to break the curse of fatherlessness off of this generation.

PARENTING
CULTIVATING IDENTITY AND PURPOSE IN OUR CHILDREN

By Tony & Nicole Davis

What the Numbers Reveal

There is a West African proverb that says, "The ruin of a nation begins in the homes of its people." If there is ANY truth to this proverb, it can be argued that the current state of our nation (the United States) is a direct reflection of what is occurring in our homes.

Here are some startling statistics to consider. In September 2017, *A Real Clear Politics* poll revealed that only 32 percent of Americans believe the country is going in the right direction.[1] A *Gallup* poll from May 2017, rating moral values in the United States, shows that 45 percent of Americans believe our values are poor, and 77 percent believe our moral values are getting worse. In the same study, when Americans were asked what has caused the moral decline, *poor parenting* was rated among the top three reasons.[2] Another study conducted by *FaithIt Inc.* shows 59 percent of millennials who were raised in church are choosing to stop attending it after the age of 18.[3] And, *Barna* research indicates that, "Most young people admit that they feel as if they do not receive sufficient attention from their parents; do not have enough good friends whom they can count on; are unsettled about their own future; have personal spiritual perspectives but not much of a sense of spiritual community; lack role models; and do not feel that they have intrinsic value."[4] These statistics paint a bleak picture; BUT, there is still hope!

We consider the Family Mountain to be the most critical of the Seven Mountains. Why? The answer is two-fold. First, it is an unavoidable mountain where everyone automatically participates. Second, every other mountain is comprised of people who belong to families. In essence, we believe strong families will produce integral people who can later positively influence the other mountains. Conversely, weak families produce anemic, dysfunctional people who can also influence these same mountains--but with negative outcomes. The statistics above validate this conclusion.

Demanding Different

Despite growing up in separate regions of the country (Tony in Baltimore, MD- Nicole in Akron, OH), our backgrounds were similar yet different. Both homes lacked affluence. Tony, the younger of two, was raised in Church; Nicole, the eldest of three, was not. Tony's paternal relationship entailed an absentee father. Nicole's father was around when expedient for his own needs. We both had mothers who *did the best they could with what they had*. That meant we were loved. Yet, extensive and continuous conversations regarding identity and future possibilities were not commonplace in either home. As a result, neither of us understood our individual capability and impact potential. Notwithstanding these facts, we strongly felt a hunger for better lives and we were determined to create different futures for ourselves—and our children.

Discipleship Begins at Home

Regarding our children, we were guided by Genesis 1:26 and Proverbs 22:6. The biblical concept that purports we are created in the image of God is often quoted; however, it's not often believed. As a result, we grow up not realizing that we really are kings and queens made in the image of God. By and large, we live in a world of dysfunction that will only change when we resume our pre-ordained places and walk fully in our Christ-like identity. And, like many parents, we look to Proverbs 22:6, that reads, "Train up a child in the way he should go, and when he is old he will not depart from it."

Traditionally, this scripture has been used to teach that training up a child simply means teach them the Word of God for the purpose of "getting it in them." The belief is that if you do this, they will eventually "come back to the Lord" when (not IF) they stray. For years, our challenge with this prevailing interpretation has been us seeing far too many Bible-believing people "stray" then die before they could "find their way back to the Lord." Fortunately for us, over the years, God has illuminated this scripture in different ways and has revealed a deeper meaning that can revolutionize the way mothers and fathers choose to parent.

In this context, the Hebrew meaning of *train up* means to initiate or instruct a child in the way *he* should go. Bible scholars denote that this does not mean just in accordance to general principles of education, moral, and spiritual guidance, but more specifically a thoughtful, intentional observation of character and capacity, with a focus on the individual course of life for *that* child. For further clarity, this type of training does not stop at a certain age, but is tailored throughout the development of the child to ensure unique exposure to opportunities that will help transform him/her into the best version of him/herself at adulthood.

To our amazement, additional study of the term *disciple* aligns greatly with this form of training. The word *disciple* means a learner or pupil. Jesus exemplified the kind of effort training required during His years with His new *babe-like* disciples. As pupils, they needed a certain kind of training to discover their true identity and purpose for the advancement of the Kingdom. And, even though they all graduated to achieve amazing things, at their core, they remained disciples (or learners).

How we parent will change as our children grow, but the fact that we parent does not. The misnomer is that the older children get, the less they need us. It is actually just the opposite. We should naturally go from teaching them the difference between colors, counting, and when to use common courtesies, to helping them establish practical responses to peer pressure, drugs, sex, alcohol, and relationships (both friendly associations and romantic pursuits). Educational guidance also intensifies as our children are faced with financial decisions and career choices as young adults. The takeaway is this: parental guidance will be needed as our children grow; and, we are responsible for training up our children with methods commensurate with *discipleship.*

What's the compelling argument? The word *train* only appears in the KJV Bible three times and none of the meanings are the same; however, the word *disciple* appears twenty-nine times and the meaning is always alike. The uniformity of definition for the term *disciple* shows a more consistent, dedicated, and result-oriented approach to the end goal of preparing a person for the future. In addition, there is an obligation to educate and demonstrate God's Word, which requires parents to exemplify what they teach just as Jesus has done for us.

The vital revelation is that discipling our children is an integral part of parenting. In fact, they are our primary discipleship assignment! So, the question you may want to ask yourself is, "If not ME, then who should be discipling MY children?" We fully acknowledge that financial prosperity has many advantages to assist in this endeavor. Nevertheless, this is not a money issue. The issues are identity and purpose. Therefore, take heart; accurate application of the Scriptures will fully equip you for this task.

As parents, we need to better understand, accept, and embrace our roles as stewards, guides, and teachers. With these terms in mind, we have much work to do to prepare our children for Kingdom influence—not just church attendance. We need a paradigm shift in our mentality about parenting and the obligation to appropriately equip our children to live godly, successful, accomplished lives, all to the Glory of God. If we can encourage parents to attack parenting from this perspective, each mountain will be overtaken by men and women who are adequately prepared to take that mountain for Jesus!

The seriousness of our role is soberly conveyed when Jesus spoke to the disciples about children in Matthew 18:5-7. We consider this admonishment to be applicable to parenting as well. With a focus on discipling our children, we will build better relationships with them and earn their respect. Inevitably, our hearts get turned towards them, and ultimately their hearts will be turned towards us as prophesied in Malachi 4:6.

To effectively train up and disciple our children, we must observe them and help develop the gifts, talents, and calling that God has already placed in them. They are not merely blank slates waiting for us to impart some great knowledge and direction to them, or to demand they pursue the dreams or intentions we have for them. We have to discern and make sure that each child is going in the way *he/she* should go; not the way we want them to go. According to Scripture, purpose had already been assigned before they were formed in their mother's womb (Jeremiah 1:5-7, Psalm 71:6). And, they can and should walk in their individual calls (Ephesians 4:1). Make no mistake, parenting done right is hard work!

Church and Family Partnership

The church can help by partnering with parents to bring prophetic insight to our children regarding God's plans for them: speaking specifically to their identity and His purpose regarding the Seven Mountains. A practical approach is for churches to provide children opportunities to enhance their gifts, talents, and abilities for a cause greater than themselves. For example, children who have demonstrated a proclivity to the health professions may be granted an opportunity to participate in ministries at hospitals and nursing homes (yes, this may require partnering with churches that are not your home one). We must be intentional in focusing our children's inherent need to thrive and find meaning in EVERY area of life—spirit, soul, and body.

Church leaders and family members need to speak into our children by the wisdom and Spirit of God (1Corinthians 2: 10-16). Remember, death and life are in the power of the tongue (Proverbs 18:21). Our children are watching and listening. What are they hearing in our communications? Are we using the power of our words to breathe life into them? Or, are we using our words to tear them down or induce fear and limited thinking? Does the church encourage them to be who they were created to be by God's design? Or does the church create an environment that brings condemnation against any desire to pursue a mountain that's not directly associated with them? We must protect our children from words, attitudes, environments, and associations that are not speaking to the king or queen inside of them.

Declarations and Prayer Points

1. I have the mind of Christ and receive revelation daily to walk according to His Kingdom principles. (Genesis 1:26 NKJV)
2. I walk in the fear and counsel of God's Word to teach my children of His goodness. (Deuteronomy 4:9-10)
3. I instruct my children to love God and honor Him in every area of life. (Deuteronomy 6:5-9)
4. I discipline my children with godly wisdom so that they may prosper.
5. (Proverbs 19:18 NLT)
6. I read the Bible to provide sound godly instruction to my children. (Proverbs 1:8-9 NKJV)
7. I declare words of life over my children to build them up. (Proverbs 18:21 MSG)
8. My heart and spirit are open to discover God's purpose for my child. (Proverbs 29:18 KJV)
9. I walk in God's strength so that I am a righteous example before my children. (Matthew18:5-6 NKJV)
10. I speak God's purpose over my children and pray for the full manifestation of God's calling. (Ephesians 4:1)
11. I exemplify a heart of a giver and a doer to show my children how to serve others. (Titus 3:14 NKJV)

Parental Decree

I am a Kingdom parent equipped to disciple my child according to knowledge and wisdom. I walk in revelation concerning the gifts and abilities of my child(ren) to expose (him/her/them) to opportunities for greater development beyond my capabilities. I will not allow society to dictate how I train and disciple my child(ren). I walk in love and faith and use my words to speak life, power, and direction. I teach my child(ren) the ways of the Lord, and exemplify a righteous lifestyle for (him/her/them) to follow. I have open communication with (him/her/them) to make sure (he/she/they) understand(s) the benefits of making good decisions. I protect my child(ren) from ungodly people sent to corrupt (his/her/their) character and sabotage (his/her/their) purpose. I decree my child(ren) will know (his/her/their) identity in Christ and will fulfill (his/her/their) God-given assignment on this Earth with my guidance and support.

---

[1] Gallup. (2017, May). Ratings of U.S. moral values. *Moral Issues*. Retrieved from http://www.gallup.com/poll/1681/moral-issues.aspx

[2] Real Clear Politics (2017, May). Direction of our country. *Poll*. Retrieved from https://www.realclearpolitics.com/epolls/other/direction_of_country-902.html

[3] Eaton, S. (2017, February). 59 Percent of millennials raised in a church have dropped out—and they're trying to tell us why. *FaithIt*. Retrieved from http://faithit.com/12-reasons-millennials-over-church-sam-eaton/

[4] Barna Research Group. (2007, April). Virginia tech tragedy is a wake-up call to parents. *Culture & Media*. Retrieved from https://www.barna.com/research/virginia-tech-tragedy-is-a-wake-up-call-to-parents/

GENERATIONAL BONDAGE AND CURSES

By Anita Etta

Your ancestors may be long gone but did you know that the things they did are still affecting your life today? The choices made by your great-grandparents are still speaking into your life. Your battles with poverty and lack could very well be due to an ancestor who cheated their workers. Your battles with sickness could be from a bloodline curse due to an ancestor who practiced witchcraft. This is a biblical principle that many Christians overlook but one that explains many of our seemingly unanswered prayers. Blessings and curses can be generational. David's blessings followed Solomon and so did his weaknesses with women. The Abrahamic blessings were generational and pronounced by God over the generations (Genesis 15:18; 17:1-6), and so were the curses that resulted from disobedience (Genesis 12:3).

This same principle is seen in Adam's sin affecting mankind (Romans 5:12), bringing about a curse that still applies to every human being, 6000 years later, except for those who enter into covenant with Christ. In Christ, generations are blessed through salvation. This is a biblical principle that works for good and evil. Romans 5:18 reveals that by one man, sin came and by one man, salvation came to humanity. What did your ancestors do that are today causing you to walk in blessings or in curses?

Although God has given us spiritual blessings in heavenly places, we may not be experiencing the manifestation of these blessings in the physical because of a curse which has put us in demonic bondage. *"A curse without cause will not alight"* (Proverbs 26:2). How then, does the devil succeed in establishing a curse in our lives? He always employs the same strategy he used on Eve, by deception and convincing us to believe him rather than God, and we enter into agreement with him of our own freewill. He lies to us by presenting us with a choice of who to believe. Our choices result in the manifestation of blessings or curses, and these will follow our generations, putting us and our children in bondage (Exodus 20:5).

The Bible makes references to *generational curses* (Exodus 20:5; 34:7; Numbers 14:18; Deuteronomy 5:9). God warns that He is "a jealous God, punishing the children for the sin of the fathers to the third and fourth generation of those who hate me." Lamentations 5:7 states, "Our fathers have sinned, and are not; and we have borne their iniquities."

For many years, I could not understand why I faced many unsurmountable obstacles with my health, finances, education, career, and so many other areas of my life, until the Lord revealed that I was dealing with generational bondage. The consequences were very detrimental, no matter how much I prayed and fasted, until the Lord redeemed me from these inherited bondages. By their action, our forefathers signed a contract for future generations. We inherit those evil covenants and pay the price. The same principle applies to blessings; due to our parents' actions, we inherit godly covenants and enjoy generational blessings. An example is the case of Solomon, who was disobedient but because of God's covenant with his father, David, who obeyed Him, Solomon still enjoyed the blessing and the curse was postponed to future generations (1 Kings 11:12). This spiritual heritage explains why people we may consider bad seem to be living a blessed life. It is like a baton passed on from generation to generation. Like a time-release capsule, these blessings and curses can also be activated at key milestones in life and transferred at the death of a parent.

Bondages and curses come into our lives through a legal right. A curse without cause will not alight, therefore if there is a curse in our lives, permission was given by us or our forefathers. Sin creates an open door, giving the devil the legal right to come into our lives to steal, kill, and destroy (John 10:10). What our ancestors did will affect us spiritually and what we do will affect our future generations. Lamentations 5:7 states, "Our fathers sinned, and are no more; It is we who have carried their sin."

Generational bondages and curses are transferred through bloodlines across various generations and have a significant impact on the family mountain. The family is the foundation of society and the extent to which the family is spiritually healthy determines the type of society we live in. Many of the ills we witness in the secular world and in the Church (including in the pulpit) are because many are still suffering from generational curses that have never been identified and addressed. Many tongue-talking, saved believers who truly love the Lord have been unable to overcome many issues because they lack understanding of this biblical principle. Hosea 4:6 says, *"My people are destroyed for lack of Knowledge.* Proverbs 11:9 says, *"...through knowledge shall the just be delivered."* Where there is bondage, there must be deliverance for the believer to walk in freedom (Obadiah 1:17). How then, does the believer identify the need for deliverance?

Generational bondages and curses can be identified by discernment and by recognizing negative patterns in multiple family members across different generations. Deuteronomy 28 reveals many of the curses experienced due to sin. Let's look at some common family patterns and cycles that may indicate generational curses:

- Continual financial difficulties which are hard to overcome thereby resulting in poverty and lack (Deuteronomy 28:17, 47-48)
- Hereditary illnesses or health conditions which Doctors are unable to diagnose although the patient has tormenting symptoms (Deuteronomy 28:21,27)
- Emotional instability including irrational fears, mental illnesses including depression, schizophrenia, and mind confusion (Deuteronomy 28:28)
- Barrenness, female problems, and other reproduction issues (Deuteronomy 28:18)
- Family breakdown and divorce. (Deuteronomy 28:30,41)
- Lack of vision and direction in life (Deuteronomy 28:29)

How to Overcome Generational Bondage

Generational bondage can only be overcome in Christ Jesus. Galatians 3:13, states that "Christ hath redeemed us from the curse of the law, being made a curse for us..." Being saved guarantees Heaven but not the quality of our lives if we are connected to evil covenants. We must apply the Word of God to break these evil covenants and walk towards our divine destiny.

Deliverance from bondage is the children's bread (Matthew 15:26) and therefore is meant only for believers in Christ. Obadiah 1:17 states that there shall be deliverance and holiness on Mt. Zion. This indicates that one cannot walk in the freedom that deliverance brings outside of a life in Christ. Although it is only by grace that deliverance is obtained in Christ, holiness closes the open doors and ensures there are no legal rights given to the devil. First, we must come to Christ and receive salvation, next we must repent of our sins and those of our forefathers (Leviticus 26:40), then we must confess and denounce all sin and turn away from our wicked ways (2 Chronicles 7:14). We must live a consecrated life (Romans 12:1-2). In Deuteronomy 30:1-3, God promises to remove the curses of Deuteronomy 28 which we may have inherited, if we are obedient. Jeremiah 31:29-30 states, *"In those days they shall say no more, the fathers have eaten sour grapes, and the children's teeth are set on edge."* Ezekiel 18:2-3 reveals God's desire to set a believer free from generational curses. In Christ, we are set free (John 8:36). Although the blood of Jesus has paid for our sins, any bondage established before the believer accepted Christ needs to be handled, and spirits enforcing this bondage must be cast out. Demons do not automatically leave when we accept Christ; they can remain dormant until certain critical times in your life. Repentance and a consecrated life of righteousness in Christ is the prerequisite for freedom from generational bondage (Romans 12:1-2).

As you dive deeply into the Word of God and seek Him, you will begin to experience the power that lies in the Word and presence of God. Darkness will begin to dispel and you will be transformed. If you are dealing with generational bondage, know that God gives grace to the afflicted

(Proverbs 3:34). While repentance, renunciation of sin, and a consecrated life are key, it is by the grace of God that we are delivered and only by His grace can our deliverance be maintained. Jesus came to set the captives free. Redemption is by the blood of Jesus and the forgiveness we receive when we repent is only made possible by the riches of God's grace (Ephesians 1:7). Apply the word of God and watch the power therein bring about your deliverance from generational bondages by separating you from the spirits of darkness that held you captive (Hebrews 4:12).

Prophetic Declarations and Prayers

- I repent of and denounce my sins and those of my forefathers who have provided a legal right for demonic bondage in my life. In Christ, I am a new creation and therefore formally being a lawful captive, now I am delivered and set free in Jesus' name (Isaiah 49:24-26).
- I repent of the sins of .... (list any sins you are aware of).
- I renounce all evil covenants that I consciously or unconsciously entered into (name those you are aware of).
- I destroy all evil altars speaking against my destiny by the blood of Jesus and fire of the Holy Spirit.
- I declare that I shall no more suffer generational bondage because of the sins of my forefathers. I have been washed with the blood of Christ and walk in obedience in Jesus' name. (Jeremiah 31:29-30).
- Oh Lord, contend with my contenders as you promised, in the name of Jesus (Isaiah 49:25).
- I command my oppressors to feed on their own flesh and be drunk of their own blood in the name of Jesus (Isaiah 49:26).
- I decree and declare that the snares in my life are all broken by the power in the blood of Jesus and that I have escaped as a bird from the fowler's snare in the name of Jesus (Psalms 124:7).
- I break every curse of .... (speak out every curse you have identified such as sickness, poverty, barrenness, and emotional instability) over my life and I nail them to the cross. I declare that henceforth I walk in.... (speak out blessings of health, prosperity, fruitfulness, a sound mind, and so on) in Jesus' name. I shall prosper

even as my soul prospers (3 John 1-2).
- I am redeemed from the curse through Christ and henceforth, I walk in complete freedom from all generational curses (Galatians 3:13).
- I blot out every handwriting of ordinances against me, including those inherited from my ancestors that are contrary to the will of God for my life. I nail them to the cross, and I forbid them from pursuing me and my future generations in Jesus' name (Colossians 2:14).
- Because I am in Christ, I receive deliverance, I walk in holiness and I possess my possessions (Obadiah 1:17).

I declare that by the blood of Jesus, I am in covenant with Christ Jesus and henceforth I am set free from all generational curses and bondage; I walk in newness of life in Christ Jesus because he who the Son sets free is free indeed! (John 8:36)

ERADICATING THE SPIRIT OF POVERTY IN OUR FAMILIES

By Sarafia Jones-Hall

Poverty is a state of economic defiance characterized by the lack of capacity to obtain the necessities of life or material comforts. According to the U.S. Census Bureau, September 2017, of a total of 319.9 million inhabitants in the U.S., 40.6 million Americans lived in poverty in 2016. Among racial and ethnic groups, African-Americans had the highest poverty rate, 27.4%, followed by Hispanics at 26.6%, and whites at 9.9%. 45.8% of young black children (under age 6) live in poverty, compared to 14.5% of white children. These numbers are much higher across the globe accumulatively. Poverty's effects have no consideration or respect of person. The unfortunate thing about individuals that experience poverty is they often blame their circumstances on the Lord rather than the real culprit—Satan. Poverty, along with this type of thinking, causes a lack of access to the open doors God has set before us.

Born Into Poverty

As I grew up, I watched how my grandmother struggled to take care of us. I thought to myself, "That will never be me." I made a promise to myself that, when I got older, I would take care of my family. Today, a flashback comes to me when our water was off for months and we had to shamefully borrow water from neighbors to bathe and flush the toilet. My grandfather worked but would get drunk and deplete all his funds. Yet, my grandmother worked two jobs and still could not provide for our basic needs. At the prime of my life, I find myself at times immobilized by poverty's ill effects. I have been fighting this demon since birth. Poverty, oh enemy of deceit, I am here today to serve you notice, you lived and died with my grandmother, grandfather, and many of my ancestors, but you will not die with me.

Unmasking the Mountain of Poverty in Families

Poverty can affect anyone, regardless of family, race, gender, culture, or religion. This monster has come to kill, steal, and destroy our families. It desires to stop, block, and corrupt God's purpose and command. Poverty is the exact opposite of God's plan for our lives. *"And God blessed them, and God said unto them, Be fruitful, and multiply, and replenish the earth, and subdue it: and have dominion over the fish of the sea, and over the fowl of the air, and over every living thing that moved upon the earth. And God said, Behold, I have given you every herb bearing seed, which is upon the face of all the earth, and every tree, in the which is the fruit of a tree yielding seed; to you it shall be for meat"* (Genesis 1:28-29 KJV).

The spirit of poverty has slithered its way into the bloodline of many families. How did this spirit get here? It came through hard hits, unexpected situations, and generational cycles passed down from our ancestors. Some knew how to survive and others did not. However, those who knew how to fight against this destitution did not share with those connected to the family tree. Therefore, the entire legacy is impacted.

Spiritual Doors and Curses of Poverty

Poverty stunts growth, which opens doors for other spirits and curses to come upon us. Concisely, it is the lack of the basic things needed to function and be a part of society. When these needs go unmet, people turn to ungodly devices. Our nation is reflective of this monstrosity, as statistics point to the high number of the poor and homeless, personal and family debt, unemployment rates, depression, divorce, murder, and suicide.

Once a victim of poverty, I can attest to several curses and doors being open. My grandmother suffered from mental illness. In 2011, she lived in another city, among family. My family did their best to aid my grandmother, but due to addiction and lack of basic needs for herself, they could not fully assist. I wanted to bring my grandmother home and care for her. However, because of the spirit of poverty over my bloodline, it was hard for me to get on my feet and save money to relocate her. My grandmother dissipated quickly and when I finally gathered the finances to visit, she died. I did not make it to her in time. It was at this moment I took revenge on poverty and made a stand to eradicate its plans from here on out.

Change Your Stinking Thinking
(Poverty Mentality)

As I began to research on poverty, I came across a statement from President Lyndon B. Johnson, who declared war on poverty in 1964. He vowed that it would not be easy. As he addressed the State of the Union, Johnson's famous proclamation is still relevant, "We shall not rest until that war is won." President Johnson is long gone and the war on poverty is still yet alive and people are fighting daily to survive.

I thank President Johnson, as I am sure many others do, for his great efforts and programs put in place to help the poor and those in lack. The program referred to as *The Great Society*, 1964, established programs such as food stamps, Medicare, Medicaid, housing, and so forth. The 1965 Housing and Urban Development Act offered grants to improve city housing and subsidized rents for the poor. The Economic Opportunity Act (EOA) of 1964 established and funded a variety of programs to assist the poor in finding jobs. All of these initiatives were substantial and initially strategic to combat poverty.

However, as I continued to study about the fight against poverty, the Lord provided a deeper insight and revelation. Even with all the programs in place to help people, many have not been ministered to or received wise counsel on how to break the cycle of lack. If there are no mental or spiritual changes, there will be no growth. People become dependent on a system and therefore will remain in an impoverished state.

The war on poverty hasn't been won, because the minds of people are dysfunctional, and they do not know how to think their way to wealth and greatness. You can give a poor person one million dollars. If they do not have the principles of the Word of God and continue to live in a poverty-stricken mindset, they will never gain and go back to bondage. The best way to wealth and wholeness is through believing what God's Word promises us and take action to change our lives.

Destroying Poverty

Many of us fell into poverty because we were told to go to college and apply for grants and loans. "Finish school, so you can get your dream job." They said we would make a lot of money; but for most of us, we created a lot of debt. The very thing we love to do was put on the back burner. Our God-given gifts and talents have not been cultivated and, instead of becoming entrepreneurs, opening up businesses, and creating family wealth, we have been operating in the wrong place.

Some have decided to give up and throw in the towel because they are unable to see the light at the end of the tunnel, but I beg to differ. The door is still there and the light is the Father who has always been there from the beginning of time. You just need to see it within yourself. From this day forward, fight the good fight of faith; from this day forth, use your gifts and abilities, sharpen your craft, and continue to perfect. The word of God tells us, *"A man's gift maketh room for him, and bringeth him before great men"* (Proverbs 18:16 KJV). We were created with a purpose, being blessed to be a blessing and build wealth for others and God's Kingdom. *"Just as you, Judah and Israel, have been a curse among the nations, so I will save you, and you will be a blessing. Do not be afraid, but let your hands be strong"* (Zechariah 8: 13 NKJV).

The spirit of poverty has controlled your life long enough! No longer shall he control you because your mind is made up, old things are passed away, and behold all things are new, in you and through you. You can and will destroy poverty.

Decree against Poverty Spirit

Poverty spirit, I decree and declare that you will *not regenerate* with *me* nor my seed. You will not go to the grave with me. I decree and declare you will go to the grave, but you will go long before me. Spirit of poverty, I come against you; by the Spirit of the living God, I speak annihilation and destruction to your very core, your root. We eradicate you now from the bloodline of my family, and all families of the faith, in the mighty name of Jesus.

Release Prayers

1. Father, I thank you that I stand under an open Heaven (Malachi 3:10).
2. Father God, thank you for restoring the years the cankerworm and the locust have eaten (Joel 2:25).
3. Surely, goodness and mercy shall follow me all the days of my life (Psalm 23:6).
4. Thank you Lord, my family and I are blessed and highly favored by you (Luke 1:28).
5. Lord, I thank you now in the name of Jesus, wealth is our portion (Proverbs 3:10).
6. Father, in the name of Jesus, I thank you that my hands are blessed, to create wealth. (Deuteronomy 28:8).
7. Thank you Lord, you are the restorer of the breach, restore all things (Matthew 17:11).
8. Thank you Lord, you are my strength and my redeemer (Psalm 19:14).
9. I thank you Lord, old things have passed away, behold all things are new in me (2 Corinthians 5:17).
10. Thank you Lord, I walk by faith and not by sight (2 Corinthians 5:7).

---

https://courses.lumenlearning.com/ushistory2os2xmaster/chapter/lyndon-johnson-and-the-great-society/

https://stateofworkingamerica.org/fact-sheets/poverty/

https://www.biblegateway.com/

PROTECTING OUR CHILDREN

By Olympia Jarboe

Guardians of the Gates

We have a responsibility to protect our children inside and outside of the womb. Parents are the spiritual gatekeepers for their children (Proverbs 22:6). Gatekeepers control what comes in and what goes out. *"The gatekeepers were stationed on all four sides — east, west, north, and south"* (1 Chronicles 9:24 New Living Translation). They allow and deny access as they see fit. What is on the inside is shielded from the dangers on the outside. Children are defenseless and vulnerable without the protection of a discerning adult. The enemy attacks our children as a way to weaken the family unit, which eventually weakens a nation.

Many broken men and women were once vulnerable children. They did not break overnight. The breaking process was gradual, the cracks were subtle, the pain was progressive, and the impact was colossal. This does not mean that their parents did not love them, neither does it mean that their parents did not try to protect them. But what it does mean is that the enemy is getting his foothold in somewhere that does not readily meet the eye. Satan is ruthlessly pursuing our children because he knows their potential. This current generation, and the ones to come, do not have to suffer needlessly. There is a solution: it is time to guard the gates!

We can switch to any news station, visit any school or hospital, or simply walk down the streets of our neighborhoods to see how our children are being challenged. They are being attacked on every side. Many of these attacks begin at the moment of conception. According to the Centers for Disease Control (2015), the top three leading causes of death for children under the age of 1 are birth defects, short gestation, and Sudden Infant Death Syndrome[1].

For children between the ages of 1 to 14, and 15 to 24, the top three include a mixture of unintentional injury, birth defects, cancer, homicide, and suicide[1]. The CDC also reports that, "nonfatal and fatal violence are substantially higher among young people than any other age group."[2] According to the Child Mind Institute (2016), mental health disorders, including learning disabilities, are the leading health issue for school-age children[3]. Also, there were an estimated 55.7 million abortions performed *each year* between 2010 and 2014[4]. I can go on with a laundry list of disheartening examples, but I trust that you see that our children are not off-limits in the devil's eyes.

The Entrances

Like Pharaoh, satan delights in oppression and rivers of blood—our children's blood (Exodus chapter 1). He seeks to kill the children and to burden their parents. He cannot tolerate the expansion of God's chief creation, *"Lest they multiply...fight against us, and so go up out of the land"* (Exodus 1:10). Neither can he stand to see us free. The enemy seeks to steal, kill, and destroy the fruits of our wombs (John 10:10). Children that are taught in the ways of the Lord are a threat to the kingdom of darkness. They are able to stand with their parents against their enemies at the gate (Psalm 127:3-5). Just as God has destined great things for our children before they were in their mother's womb (Jeremiah 1:5), so has satan plotted their demise.

It is the enemy's goal to snatch the life right out of our children before they get a chance to really live. All souls, young, old, and unborn, belong to God (Ezekiel 18:4). Do not allow yourself to be seduced by the Pharaoh spirit. Do not make the decision to throw your child into the river via abortion. Every conceived pregnancy is a life God has destined to live. Besides abortion, satan has found a way to terminate pregnancies before they come to term, or snatch lives in infancy. Note, women who desire to have children someday need to dedicate their womb and unborn children to the Lord. Hannah did it (1 Samuel 1:11). Guard the womb gate!

As a social worker, I have worked with families in a variety of settings. No parent wants to see their child murdered. In their minds, no parent wants to see their child struggle through life. No parent wants to see their child take their own life. I specifically work as a mental health consultant in my current capacity. Daily, I review cases that involve mental health concerns for both parents and children. This is where the enemy attacks, in the mind. Many children grow up in dysfunction as the intergenerational effects of trauma and stress go unmanaged. Our society is inundated with realities that can wear out the psychological fabric of a child's mind. Micro-aggressions, mass shootings, terrorist attacks, police brutality, racism, sexism, conflicting social messages, ungodly ideology, mind control TV programming, bullying, and much more continue to confuse young minds. God revealed to us that the evil imaginations of the human heart begin in our childhood (Genesis 8:21). Of course, it is impossible to shield our children from everything, but active intercession and warfare is needed. Guard their mental gate!

Many of the parents that I have worked with were overwhelmed, frustrated, or discouraged, because of the challenges they faced with their children. Although these parents were receiving assistance, they still appeared helpless. A few years ago, the Lord gave me a dream. In the dream, officials were going door to door removing people. When they got to my house, there were suddenly children in my living room. I told the officials that I was their caretaker. The officials looked at me and then looked at the children; they then reluctantly left. Silently, I stood there looking at the children and they looked at me. I observed that they were of various ages, races, ethnicities, and heights. Their eyes were full of innocence and expectation. I thought to myself, "Where are their parents?"

The Deliverer is Here

Pharaoh—satan, is no longer simply after the boys, but he wants the girls too. He wants the unborn, the infants, the toddlers, pre-teens, teens, and young adults. He even wants the parents. His plan is insidious: permeating through families, communities, churches, cities, and nations.

Over half of the abortions performed every year are potentially fatal for the mother as well, killing both mother and child. When a young person is murdered by another young person, two lives are lost to violence, and both families feel the pain. Many parents deplete their finances and endure heartache as their child suffers from cancer and other terrible diseases. The pain of burying a child is a heavy load to bear. But GOD says, "THERE IS HELP!" Just as God gave Moses' parents favor, wisdom, and courage to save their child's life (Exodus 2:1-3; Hebrews 11:23), so shall He give you! Pharaoh will pursue until he is drowned by your prayers of intercessions and warfare. Jesus wants us to bring our children to Him (Luke 18:16) for refuge; it is never too early. Cover your children even from the womb.

Declarations for Parents

1. I am the spiritual gatekeeper for my child(ren), and the Lord is with me (1 Chronicles 9:20 NLT).
2. I am not ignorant of satan's devices (2 Corinthians 2:11).
3. I give unto the Lord all the children of my womb (my wife's womb) (Exodus 13:15).
4. I declare that the Lord is a refuge for my children (Proverbs 14:26 NLT).
5. I declare that my child(ren) shall not be killed or thrown into the river (Exodus 1:16, 22).
6. I will discipline my child(ren) while there is hope, in order to save his/her life (Proverbs 19:18 NLT).
7. I declare that my child(ren) shall have peace of mind and peace of body.
8. I declare that every enemy or offense will be drowned in the sea for my children's sake (Matthews 18:6).
9. I declare that my child shall not die by his/her own hand, or by the hand of another.
10. I sanctify my offspring with the blood of Jesus (Exodus 13:2); Lord, surround them with your warrior, guardian, and ministering angels.

Decree for Parents

I decree that the fruit of my body is blessed (Deuteronomy 28:4). God has made me to laugh (Genesis 21:6), because He has kept barrenness from me. He has remembered me, heard me, and opened my womb (Genesis 30:22). My children are protected in the mighty name of Jesus. For when the enemy shall come in like a flood, the Spirit of the Lord shall lift up a standard against him (Isaiah 59:19). My child is a goodly child (Exodus 2:2), and I hide him/her under the shadow of the Almighty (Psalm 91:1). I decree that no harm or danger shall come nigh them (Psalm 91:7). My children shall be taught of the Lord, and their peace shall be great (Isaiah 54:13). My children are my heritage; the fruit of my womb is my reward (Proverbs 127:3). My children's children are my crown, and I am the glory of my children (Proverbs 17:6). I decree that my child shall not die before his/her time, but live, and declare the works of the Lord (Psalm 118:17).

---

[1] https://www.cdc.gov/injury/wisqars/pdf/leading_causes_of_death_by_age_group_2015-a.pdf

[2] https://www.cdc.gov/healthcommunication/toolstemplates/entertainmented/tips/violenceyouth.html

[3] https://childmind.org/report/2016-childrens-mental-health-report/

[4] http://www.cnn.com/2017/09/27/health/abortion-safety-global-study/index.html

THE RESTORATION OF THE FAMILY UNIT

By Christine Cline

God has ordained and instituted family. The devil hates family and tries his best to divide and destroy what God has created. Before God established the Church, He established the family unit. "Strong families create strong communities. Strong communities build strong cities. Strong cities build strong states, which in turn has the potential of building strong countries, and from the strong countries, strong nations are to follow," I can hear my pastor, Johnny Brown, state so eloquently.

Throughout the Bible, from Genesis to Revelation, it is seen that Satan is opposed to the Word and will of God, and he's determined to pervert and prevent God's plan, starting with the first family. In the temptation of Adam and Eve (Genesis 3:1-5), the fall of man occurs, bringing about separation and division.

Exemplifying Godly Relationships in the Home

We were purposefully crafted by God for unity, fellowship, oneness, and relationship. God's original design for us did not include breakups. *"Therefore shall a man leave his father and his mother, and shall cleave unto his wife: and the two shall become one flesh"* (Genesis 2:24). Breakups contradict God's design for oneness. Broken relationships open portals for perversion, and distorts the reflection of God's original design for family. What therefore God hath joined together, let not man put asunder (Mark 10:9).

Better Together

Infiltrating sin rots the core of God's ordained family sectors. Keeping in mind that a family is comprised of a household, often parents and children, every choice and action, known or unknown affects every individual to some degree within that family unit. Protecting the structure of that house relies strongly on prayer and applying the word of God in every situation to keep that family rooted and grounded.

Giving God the leading role in our household is vital to the success and function of a healthy, thriving family. With God as the Head, husband, wife, and their children will live in harmony. With God's counsel and leading, we cannot control or abuse others, as we will be given to love and faithfulness to Christ, and by extension, to our spouse and children. And we will ever seek to walk according to God's original design for the family, and not division. The devil only comes to steal, kill, and destroy; so he is seeking to destroy family values in society. Never let him in.

God's design for the family is that:

1. Husbands love their wives and not be harsh to them (Ephesians 5:25).
2. Wives submit to their husbands (Ephesians 5:22).
3. Children obey their parents in everything (Ephesians 6:1).
4. Parents not embitter their children (Ephesians 6:4).

Devastating Effects of Sin on the Family

Becoming a young, unwed mother at the age of 19, I can view in retrospect many errors, as the result of rebellion and sin. The third eldest of eight children, raised in church, fed the Word morning, noon, and night, yet I fell victim to the indulgences of my own fleshy desires. There was a longing or a void in me due to a broken relationship with my biological father from my early youth.

The cycle continued from generation to generation, tracing back to his grandparents. Sin that is not dealt with can have a negative impact on future generations (Exodus 20:5). Time does not heal all wounds, and suppressed issues from the past don't just disappear, they simply evolve and reappear later in life. Repentance and restoration are the determining factors that will shift the paradigm of one's life. Working primarily in the field of education, and secondarily as a caregiver, as well as active in ministry, I've been fortunate to experience various elements of "family life." Some better than others, but the ultimate facet that I have noted is that those families under the leadership of Christ are the most dynamic. Family drama does not have to stop God's plan for you.

The Family Unit is Under Attack

Media play a major role in undermining the family. The message of much of today's music is degrading to females, portraying them as sex objects for satisfying male lust. TV sitcoms and movies glorify the single life. However, when married characters are portrayed, usually the husband is depicted as an inept bumbler while the wife rules the home, heightening role-reversal of the family; not the will of God. Children are often shown as know-it-alls who mock and insult their parents. TV and movie screenwriters are constantly exposing sex, nudity, profanity, demasculinization of men, and perversion. Meanwhile, our governments have compromised and advocated policies that undermine families as they redefine marriage, penalize traditional marriage through higher taxes, advocate sex outside of marriage, reward promiscuity and single motherhood, and teach children distorted family roles. Such a sustained assault on families!

Consider that the Bible refers to our day as "this present evil age" (Galatians 1:4). It further reveals that an evil being whom it calls "the god of this age" (2 Corinthians 4:4) has blinded the minds of people, and "the whole world lies under the sway of the wicked one" (1 John 5:19) "who deceives the whole world" (Revelation 12:9). Satan is constantly waging war on families and wants to blind humankind to God's true purpose for families, but we as believers have been equipped to fight back. We must take dominion and rule God's way.

We are enlightened according to 2 Corinthians 10:4, *"For the weapons of our warfare are not carnal, but mighty through God to the pulling down of strongholds."* Ephesians 6:12 states, *"For we wrestle not against flesh and blood, but against principalities, against powers, against the rulers of the darkness of this world, against spiritual wickedness in high places."*

Use what you've got! God's word prevails and avails much, so grab a hold of the altar, travail in the Spirit, refuse to be pitiful, and be strong in the Lord.

Prayer is a Weapon of Mass Destruction Against the Kingdom of Darkness

Father of Heaven and of Earth, we thank you. Lord God, we bless your holy name, for you alone are worthy and just to exceed our expectations. So, God, with a glad heart, we lift up a praise. Lord, we bless you in the beauty of your holiness. Let your presence fill this place. Holy Spirit, you are welcome. I welcome you into every area of my life. Have your way, God. Permeate the very essence of my home. Saturate the atmosphere, dear God, and arrest the hearts that reside within this dwelling.

I ask that you open the eyes of our heart, dear God, and redirect our posture, so that we can see you with full understanding and be fully receptive to you, Oh God. Lead, guide, direct, and protect us. Continue to order our steps, my God, as you are a lamp unto our feet, and a light unto our path. Make every crooked path straight as you order our steps, heavenly Father. Forgive us for the times that we have tried to go before you and refused to submit.

Lord, forgive our very thought, word, and deed that has not lined up to your Word and will for our lives. Jesus, the same way that we ask and receive forgiveness from you, we too extend forgiveness to our offenders. Create within us a clean heart, and renew a right spirit. Lord, teach us to love you as we should, for your Word says, "If we love you, then we'll obey you." So God, teach us obedience.

I anoint myself, my children, and my spouse from the crown of our heads to the soles of our feet. Lord God, I thank you that the very hairs of our head, you have numbered. Lord, protect our gateways that allow access to our soul. Keep us that our soul doesn't taint our spirit-man.

Lord, touch our mouths and put your Word in them. Protect our spiritual gateways that when we pass through environments and enter atmospheres, we aren't infiltrated from outside distractions and demonic influences. Safeguard our hearts, Oh God, as we surrender them unto you. Bless our arms to carry the weight of our calling. Anoint our hands to be a blessing and bring glory to your name. Strengthen our legs to stand strong in the Lord and in the power of your might.

Dear God, order our steps, that everywhere the soles of our feet shall tread upon we can claim victory. I ask that all sin residue be purged from the core of our souls and that you, God, seal our lives in Christ Jesus. I appropriate the blood of Jesus over our very lives, that we may live our everyday lives according to your will, and untimely death shall not befall us. Deliver us from old mindsets, so that we can be effective in your Kingdom. As we bless your holy name, we say thank you for the keeping, reestablishing, and raising up of our families. This we pray in the name that is above all names; Jesus! Thank you, Lord God. Amen.

Declarations and Decrees

Job 22:28 states, *"Thou shalt also decree a thing, and it shall be established unto thee: and the light shall shine upon thy ways."*

1. As for me and my house, we will serve the Lord (Joshua 24:15).
2. I speak in the authority of Jesus' name and I bind bondage in my generation, and loose peace, love, and a sound mind (Matthew 18:18).
3. I have the mind of Christ (Philippians 2:5).
4. My family will not be defeated nor depleted (Romans 8:31-39).
5. God's prophecy for me has not changed (2 Corinthians 1:20).
6. I declare and decree divine internal and external healing over my family, for healing is .the children's bread, and we are children of God (Mark 7:27)
7. I speak restoration over every area of your family: your family is restored, your identity is restored, your focus is restored, your feelings are restored, your relationships are restored, your children are restored, and your health is restored, in the name of Jesus.

All scriptures are cited from the *King James Version* (KJV), unless otherwise noted.

Pastor Johnny Brown, "Family Conference" TheGenesisChurch.com (August 2017)

Bruce Gottschee, "Marriage, God's Way Pt.2" Union Church: http://www.unionchurch/archive/091398.html (August 26, 2014).

J.F. MacArthur Jr., MacArthur New Testament Commentary: Colossians. (Chicago: Moody Press, 1992), 168.

MARRIAGE AND FAMILY

By Noreen N. Henry

Marriage was ordained by God. It is a covenant relationship that reflects the relationship between God and mankind. Marriage and family are important to God because He desires for us to be fruitful and multiply (Genesis 1:18), be happy, and have a positive and godly society. The beginning of the family started in Genesis 2:18 and 2:21-24.

I was married, but due to a lack of knowledge (Hosea 4:6), and not understanding the importance of my marriage vows, I filed for divorce. My husband left one weekend and never returned.

The Bible clearly states that we become one flesh when we are married, meaning we are to be married for life. For marriage to be the way God intended, we need to focus on God and seek Him first (Matthew 6:33 and Luke 12:31). In doing this, we will see things from God's perspective and we will do right towards our spouses—and children, if any.

Husbands' and Wives' Roles

The Bible is our guide for living; it reveals how husbands and wives are to be with one another. As we take heed to the Scriptures, we will have marriages the way God intended. The following Scriptures are for the husband and wife to abide by: Ephesians 5:22-25, 5:28-29, 5:33.

A big part of the problem is the attack on men. The enemy mounts a sustained attack against men because he knows the importance of their role in marriage, in the lives of their children, and ultimately their impact on society. In order for this to change, men have to learn their roles from God's perspective and be who God has called them to be. This way, they will be in their rightful places in their family and also in society, thereby producing positivity in society.

God Hates Divorce

Malachi 2:16 confirms this truth. Why does God hate divorce? Divorce often comes from living outside the will of God. My marriage was on a downward spiral because of not being in God's will. Negativity is produced by not doing the will of God. The main thing was, *not knowing His will*. As the Word of God says, we perish for lack of knowledge (Hosea 4:6), and my marriage really did perish because of lack of knowledge. If my husband and I had been rooted in the Word of God, and serious in our relationship with the Lord, negative things could have been prevented. From my experience, I have learned that God hates divorce, because of the negative impact it has on everyone involved. When my marriage relationship was no more, the devastating effects did not show at first. It was about a year later that the effects of the sin and divorce started to affect us.

Divorce causes confusion. Children get confused, not knowing who to trust. My children didn't know if they should trust their father or me. Another thing that divorce can cause is separation anxiety. "Separation Anxiety Disorder is a clinical term that describes an extreme state of distress that's experienced when a person is separated from someone they're close to; like a mother or a father, that is more common with divorced parents" (Excerpt from *Psychology today, Divorce and Separation Anxiety*).

Children Need Their Fathers

After my husband was gone, I began to recognize the negative effects that our break-up had on my household. I started saying to myself, "If Bert was here, this wouldn't be happening." It took me a few years to realize that the issues I started to have with my children were due to their father not being there. Because of my experience, I know that the issues I've dealt with, in relation to my children, wouldn't have been that way if my husband was there. Children suffer a great deal when abandoned, and if not dealt with properly, the effects can last a lifetime.

What I realized as well was, even though my children had me, it wasn't enough. With their father showing that he didn't care about them, by leaving the way he did, they subconsciously thought, "My parent doesn't care about me, so why should I care about myself?" Studies show that children care less about themselves when a parent abandons them and are likely to commit *self-sabotage*. I can attest to this because I have lived it.

[Excerpt from the article *Consequences of Child Abandonment & Neglect*:] "The consequences of a child's neglect and abandonment are huge and unimaginable. It has created emotionally starved children in America who are confused and unstable, and will suffer lasting psychological effects." This shows that there are devastating effects on the children of an absent parent.

I've encountered many instances that showed me why their father was needed; why two-parent homes are important. It makes a huge difference. My children began to listen to me less, and I know that if their father was there, it wouldn't have been that way.

People need to realize the dire effects of divorce and abandonment. Many think it is okay to walk away from their families, but do not consider the aftermath that follows.

There are multiple statistics on matters relating to marriage and divorce. For instance, statistics show children from broken homes are more likely to drop out of school, and two of my children did. Broken homes produce broken children that become broken adults. Unless a person is strong and stable, there will be negative results from a broken home.

God gave us standards to live by, which will prevent all this hurt and pain if we abide by them. God's standards are to protect us from hurt and pain, and if we live by His standards, there won't be so much hurt, anger, bitterness, etc. that we see in today's marriages. We would make right choices for a happy life for all.

It is important to take marriage and family seriously and do what's right in order for children to be secure and happy, the way God intended. It is important for both men and women to be in their rightful places with their family and for the men to be the head as God ordained (Ephesians 5:21-33). This will make society much better.

Church & Marriage

One of the things that will help with marriage and family is the Church teaching the importance of marriage and how society is molded because of it. This will help people to understand the impact that marriage and family have on society and how important it is for marriages to be right and held in high esteem.

When we rightly divide and apply the Word of God, families will be intact and society will be impacted positively. I hope my experiences help to prevent divorce and abandonment in the lives of others. I pray that we take marriage and family seriously and take back our families.

Declarations, Decrees & Prayer Points

For the Married:

1. I bind, block, break, crush, and shatter every plan and plot of destruction for my marriage in Jesus' name.
2. Our three-fold cord can't be broken—God, husband, and wife.
3. My marriage is strong and built on the foundation and standards of the Lord.
4. What God has joined together, let no one separate.
5. My spouse and I are bound together until death separates us (Romans 7:1-3).
6. My spouse and I are united as one (Gen. 2:24-25).
1. 7. My husband loves me like Christ loves the Church (my wife respects me) (Eph. 5:22-28, 33).
7. I release unity and peace into my marriage, in Jesus' name.
8. My spouse and I only have eyes for one another.
9. I rejoice in the wife of my youth (Proverb 5:18).

For the Divorced:

1. I repent of divorcing
2. I bind the shame of divorce and loose the peace of God.

3. Reconciliation is better and the best way (1 Corinthians 7:11)

For the Abandoned:

1. I bind the spirit of rejection and all associated spirits of rejection in the name of Jesus and,
2. I lose the spirit of adoption. (Romans 8:15)
3. I bind all the negative effects of abandonment in Jesus' name.
4. I come against the trauma of abandonment in Jesus' name.
5. Father God, release peace to the abandoned and give your angels charge over them, ministering to them, and guarding them in Jesus' name.

SEEDS OF EDEN

By Cynthia Williams-Bey

Born to a single mother in Brooklyn NY, my experience of my father's infidelity is just a small part of where my story began. Even though I would like to imagine my childhood as one that consisted of a depiction of the "Cosbys," with a father that had the characteristics and integrity of "Bill," and a mother with the mannerism and submission of "Clair," my story was quite the opposite. See, my father was married when he and my mother embarked on their romantic journey. I was one of 19 children that were all products of my father's sin. I didn't have the perfect family or example of what it was to be a godly husband or a Proverbs 31 woman. There was no house, dog, or white picket fence with a home full of love and joy. I was surrounded by violence, dysfunction, and poverty, right in the heart of the Ghetto on one of the roughest streets in *Bed Stuy*, Brooklyn.

Growing up in a single parent home didn't unveil its face until I was 14 years old and pregnant. I became pregnant at that young age because I was looking to fill a void. To save me and keep me from shame, my pregnancy was hidden and I was sent off to a clinic in the wee hours of dawn so the evidence of my promiscuity was aborted. It was a decision that a desperate single mother had to make to try and save her youngest daughter from going down the same paths as she and her eldest daughters did. The seeds were already sown and the dysfunction had already taken root in the innermost parts of my being. The generational curse had already manifested and it would take more than a trip to the clinic to break it; we were just seeds of Eden (Genesis 3:3-6 KJV).

The moment Eve bit into the forbidden fruit, seeds of lust, gender confusion, adultery, and betrayal were planted. Many of these seeds are affecting the function of the family today and causing the covenant of marriage to lose its sacredness. However, I believe there is one major seed that many choose to overlook, and that is the illegal authority of women leading the family by way of single motherhood. According to Singlemother.com, "Single motherhood" is becoming the new norm. If single motherhood is becoming the new norm, then where does this leave our men? With who are we as women going to be fruitful and multiply if we're all single and leading our homes alone? How can we claim to be children of God if we're not keeping His commandments and following His natural order of the family?

According to the 2016 Census Bureau, 4 out of 10 children are being raised by unmarried women and 80% of these are single-parent homes. Growing up in a single parent home, I've seen firsthand how strong and resilient a woman can be when it comes to raising children on her own—and I applaud my mom for that. I also went through a season of single motherhood before I met my husband and it gave me a new respect for those that have been doing it for years.

Therefore, this is not a condemnation of single mothers, but merely an example of how the enemy is working to keep our men deposed and make our women carry this burden alone. Is this God's will? Is this what God had in mind when He structured the family? No matter how we look at it and how we attempt to justify it, the answer is no. God's will for the family was established in Genesis (Genesis 2:18-25).

According to the Bible, women were created to be the helper, not the tiller. Adam was given the charge of tilling the land. Eve's act of disobedience disrupted the natural order and, as a result, women are now subject to the voice of the enemy and of counterfeits that were never meant to know us. I know this because I fell victim to it myself and was left to deal with the seeds of my fornication. That experience left me bitter and fearful and initially caused my marriage to struggle. I didn't allow my husband to lead, and I tried my best to control everything. I had my own business, home, car, and good credit so I felt like I didn't need him because I was a strong woman. God showed me that I was operating in error; however, it still took me years to finally submit to my husband and the will of God for my life. Ironically, what I came to realize along the way is that I didn't even know how to follow; I had never learned.

Many have allowed the enemy's agenda to supersede God's original state of marriage and pervert it to please their fleshly desires. If they don't change their ways, many women will continue taking on the role of a man. There will be a movement of Eves that don't want to be under the care, love, and leadership of Adam, but rulers of the land by themselves. With fewer men in the position to protect our children and women, we will be even more susceptible to the kingdom of darkness. However, God has already given us the power and authority to intercede and overcome the enemies plan (Luke 10:19 KJV).

To start, we must first repent and ask for His forgiveness. God's desire is for us to get back to our original state and draw closer to Him. Marriage is the representation of the God and the Church (Ephesians 5:21-32 KJV).

How can we win souls and gain influence in the mountain of family if there are no Kingdom marriages reigning? God is calling us to be the example and equip our men and women so that the lost can turn away from their wicked ways and follow the proper family structure. God is raising up women in this hour who will travail for their husbands in prayer. These women will shift the atmosphere and propel our men back into their rightful position. These women will not be fooled by the devices of the enemy, and they will be able to identify counterfeits in the spirit. They will not only travail for their husbands but they will war and intercede for the women around them. They will break generational curses and cause the seeds that were meant to destroy the family to be uprooted, and they will plant God-kind seeds and bring forth a new, strong and unbreakable family unit. While the enemy used the woman as a weapon in the Garden of Eden to take our men out of position, God is going to use women to reestablish the family and operate in a new level of submission. The Word of the Lord says it's time to arise and shift back to your rightful position, woman of God. Arise, my warring daughters, arise!

Prophetic Declarations and Decrees for the Family Unit

- I decree and declare that every satanic influence that reigns in the family unit shall no longer have residence and be cast back to the pits of hell in the name of Jesus.
- I decree and declare that the seeds of Eden that were planted to disrupt the natural order of God shall be used against the enemy to reestablish and grow a stronger foundation for the family unit in the name of Jesus.
- I decree and declare that the spirit of perversion over the covenant of marriage shall be broken and dismantled in the name of Jesus.
- I decree and declare that men all over the world will resubmit their lives to God and prepare to take their rightful position on Earth and lead their families into their destined place in the name of Jesus.

Prophetic Declarations and Decrees for the Wife

- Father God, I ask you to forgive me for any time I fell short of your glory and tried to operate and change my husband with my own strength.
- Father God, I resubmit my will for your will and I ask you to put me back in proper alignment within my household and allow me to operate with grace in the position you assigned for me as a wife.
- I decree and declare that my husband is the head and not the tail and that he shall assume his rightful position in our marriage and on the Earth.
- I come against every generational curse and arrow from hell that has been assigned against my husband and family's prosperity; and I plead the blood of Jesus over the arrow and send it back to the pits of hell, in the name of Jesus.
- I decree and declare that my household will be a pillar of light on this Earth filled with the glory and presence of the Lord and surrounded by warring angels to fight against any demonic spirit or influence that may try to gain entry to my home.
- I decree and declare that our children shall not fall victim to the seeds of Eden and their innocence will be kept until they are revealed to

their God-ordained spouse, in the name of Jesus.

Prophetic Declarations and Prayer Points for Single Women

- I decree and declare that the voice of the enemy shall no longer pervert the ear gates of any single woman, in the name of Jesus.
- I decree and declare that every single woman shall be hidden under a veil until she is found by her God-sent husband, in the name of Jesus.
- I decree and declare that the burden of single mothers shall be lifted off the women of God and they shall no longer carry the family alone nor continue to birth children with counterfeits, in the name of Jesus.
- I appropriate the blood of Jesus and a barrier of protection around single mothers' households, to keep them from devil-sent men that will harm their children, in the name of Jesus.
- I decree and declare that every single woman will be given double honor for keeping the commandments of God and not falling victim to the enemy's tactics, in the name of Jesus.

CHAPTER 2

THE MOUNTAIN OF MEDIA

This mountain includes news outlets like CNN and Fox, newspapers, magazines, books, social media, and blogs. Francis Schaeffer once said, "Whoever controls the media controls the culture." The problem we have today is that most of the news we get is slanted toward a certain bias, with us only receiving a partial truth. Satan uses those under his sway on this mountain to attempt to control public opinion. He uses them to slant the news to create fear and hopelessness. There is very little "good news" on most news outlets. And look at the influence of social media today, with platforms like Facebook having over two billion people connected globally. The power of social media is stunning. Movements of youth that took to the streets to protest a few years ago, toppled oppressive governments in the Middle East, after having been ignited and energized through Twitter. Massive change can occur rapidly today through social media. An idea can now travel the globe in seconds.

Christians called to this mountain must maximize their influence through writing books, and in blogs, and building a strong social media presence. They must scale this mountain with revelation and truth. They must prepare to become positioned in places of influence in established news outlets, along with establishing new outlets. Statistics show that Millennials now get their news primarily from social media rather than the TV or Cable news establishment. News and opinion websites are growing exponentially. If we are to be salt and light Kingdom influence, we must engage and scale this Mountain of Media with wisdom and understanding, trusting God's favor to promote us as we develop and grow our platform of influence.

EXPOSING DARK POWERS & RELEASING TRUE LIGHT!

By Yolanda L. Powell

The Magnetic Power of Media on the Masses

What is the first thing most folks do when they wake up in the morning, get out of their car, or sit down before a meal? They check their cell phones. Period. Today, social media, news media, and global communications dominate our focus and hold an irresistible place over our everyday lives. We search Google for answers to our questions, stay current on daily events via Facebook, and get the latest news on Twitter. From media posts to inbox messages, shared chats, quick taps, and short tweets, we form opinions, understand trends, and download the issues affecting us personally, nationally, and globally through media. Utilizing this medium of influence, we decide what places to go, how we will vote, where we will live, and what we will wear. The media is a crucial life channel for us all. It's a magnetic draw and only a few complain about its intrusive nature within the culture. By all appearances, we're "hooked," and being "unplugged" from the 'Matrix of Media' is fast becoming an undesired option. And it will only increase.

"Interactive media, fueled by the advance of digital technology and the growing convergence of the computer, telephone and cable television, represent a principal trend of (innovation) at the end of the 20th and the beginning of the 21st centuries." The evolutionary progress of mass media in the States alone is staggering and the remainder of the world is not far behind. Therefore, we must utilize the old journalistic scale of who, what, when, where, why, and how to critically examine Media as a major social influencer. It's time to scale this vital Mountain and see the powerbrokers seated on its peak. Doing so will help us understand the elements behind this great influence in our lives, which dominates our daily movement on the planet.

Identifying the *Power Six* of Media

Based on an infographic by an industry watch-dog known as Frugal Dad, the media has never been more consolidated than now. Six media Giants now control a staggering 90% of what we read, watch, or listen to. Therefore, this monopoly has talons in full-throttled operation on this Mountain. Interestingly, this shift happened in less than two decades. In 1983, 90% of American media was owned by 50 companies. By 2011, that same 90% was controlled by only six. These six companies are known as 'The Power Six' and few know their influence:

1. **GE** - Comcast, NBC, Universal Pictures, Focus Features
2. **News Corp** – Fox, Wall Street Journal, New York Post
3. **Disney** - ABC, ESPN, Pixar, Miramax, Marvel Studios
4. **Viacom** – MTV, Nick Jr., BET, CMT, Paramount Pictures
5. **Time Warner** – CNN, HBO, Time, Warner Brothers
6. **CBS** – Showtime, Smithsonian Channel, NFL.com, Jeopardy, 60 Minutes

As you can see, the arteries of the **Power Six** run deep into every spectrum of life, work, and play. As Frugal Dad creatively outlines in his famous Infographics, "This equates to Media owners and executives controlling the information diet of 277 million Americans or 1 media outlet to 850,000 subscribers; an audience the size of San Francisco." What an eye-opener!

"In terms of revenue, the big six in 2010 totaled $275.9 billion dollars," Frugal Dad writes. "That's 36 billion more than Finland's Gross Domestic Product (GDP); or enough to buy every NFL team 13 times and 5x the government bailout of General Motors." How staggering!

The Power Six are in essence, Media Giants, who dominate this Mountain. Sadly, they were powered by FCC regulation and carefully designed by mergers and acquisitions—all supported by the government. So, how does a Kingdom Agenda penetrate this reality and invade this Mountain? First of all, we must clearly see what lurks behind these powerbrokers and their rise to the top of Media. Only then can we depose the demonic structures that feed and fertilize this domination from invisible realms.

The Ruling Principalities Behind All the Power

Once the natural is unveiled, then it's time to reveal the spiritual. According to Johnny Enlow, author of *The Seven Mountain Prophecy*, "The Mountain of media is currently occupied almost entirely by evil forces. Because we have never recognized the value of taking media outlets for the Kingdom, they have become major tools of the enemy that we must rend out of his hands. He has lived almost unopposed on this Mountain, and he has taken full advantage of its influence."

With the formation of apostolic-prophetic infusion groups like Extraordinary People Influencing Culture (EPIC), this is no longer the case. Kingdom leaders are being trained and developed to walk heavy in the five-fold gifting, and are skilled and graced to scale the Mountain of Media and deal with its ruling elements. We have lived for this day and are more informed and outfitted than any other generation of believers to make this assent. Yet, we have to clearly know the enemy operating specifically in the Media Mountain.

Through Enlow's prophetic insights, we have identified the Hittites described in Deuteronomy 7 and Apollyon outlined in Revelations 9 as the main adversarial forces of contention and opposition on this Mountain. The word *Hittite* comes from the name *Heth*, which means "fear" or "terror." News reporting is generally slanted to the dark-side and laced with fear-tactics to manipulate the viewing audience and sway public opinion.

Moreover, the ruling spirit over the Hittites is known as Apollyon, who currently occupies the top of the Mountain of Media. *Apollyon* means "destroyer" or "destruction," and that's exactly what he releases through his control of this Mountain. Those empowered by this ancient spirit are given "tails like scorpions" and possess "stings in their tails." Scorpions have forked tails—or more appropriately, forked "tales." This certainly describes the work produced by many media outlets. They are twisting news and broadcasting programming that is often harmful to the masses.

Strategy #1: The New Breed Evangelist with Beautiful Feet

Therefore, an Army of *new bread* media owners, board members, corporate executives, reporters, journalists, advertisers, and marketers must ascend this Mountain to overthrow the operating Hittites and Apollyon talebearers that rule. We have to 'think Kingdom' at a whole new level – if we are really going to be about the business of God and advancing His Kingdom on Earth on this major Mountain.

One of the primary strategies for Media reform is to train and equip an army of 'Beautiful Feet' according to Romans 10:15 which actually says, "…How beautiful [on the mountains] are the feet of those who bring good news." This release of peace, prosperity, and hope—amidst fear, lies, and terror—is vital in this hour. This primary strategy is to **Reposition Marketplace Evangelists** in their proper place of influence so that they can skillfully intercept and impact the Media Mountain. They will move outside of conference meetings and traditional church work, for they were never called to be preachers to Christians, but storytellers and recruiters to the nations. They must be totally repositioned on the Mountains of Media with the arsenal and anointing of good news!

Strategy #2: Firestorm Intercessors on the Mountains

Training and developing is our second strategy as we **Reignite Prophetic Intercessors** who will release a fire-storm of skillful, strategic, and successful war against the Hittite spirit and its tails of fear and terror; and Apollyon and his stinging scorpions of lies and destruction. A bombardment of fiery intercession with prophetic time-bombs must be released non-stop among prayer warriors called to battle this Mountain and return the airways to the King of Glory.

Strategy #3: Wealthy Financiers Stockholders at the Top

As Isaiah 2:2 indicates, "In these latter days, the mountain of the Lord's house will be exalted above the world's mountains," and the nations will excitedly run to these new manifestations of Heaven on Earth. But, there's work to do in order to see that glorious day before us.

The top of the Mountain refers to influence over millions of people in a directly sustained way. So, behind-the-scenes, wealthy financiers are obviously very key. Whoever maneuvers the monies and sets the philosophical guidelines, is the person with the real influence. So even though we invade and intercede, we must also be able to make substantial investments in order to take the Media Mountain.

Our third strategy is to **Raise Up Wealthy Financiers and Shareholders** who will combat idolatry, greed, and covetousness in order to maneuver billions of dollars through a massive portfolio of investments, commodities, stocks, and bonds. They will retake The Power Six and govern assets and dividends as righteous leaders with integrity and honor. It is Almighty God that "gives us the power to get wealth" and He wants His offspring prosperous and powerfully positioned on top of the Media Mountain, brokering deals, and expanding His influence in these realms.

Once an apostolic-prophetic plan with this kind of three-pronged strategy is in place, the Mountain will begin to quake with change and reform. Prophetic intercessors will encircle the atmosphere. Beautiful feet will scale the sides. Marketplace evangelists will inhabit the core. Wealthy Financiers will rule the top. Then we'll see great light overtake this dark Mountain; and many will be free to live, move, and have their being in Christ the King. The Seven Mountains will hear His Voice and another they will not follow. The righteous realms will be open wide and global channels of communication will flow with continuous good news.

---

[1] Wendt, T., & Spohn, A. (n.d.). The Role of Mass Media in Modern American Culture. Retrieved from https://sites.google.com/site/americanpoliticalparanoia/the-role-of-mass-media-in-american-political-culture

[2] The Culture of the United States: A Series (Edited 9 September 2017). Retrieved from https://en.wikipedia.org/wiki/Media_of_the_United_States

[3] These 6 Corporations Control 90% of the Media in America, by Wendy Lutz (4 July 2012). Infographic created by Frugal Dad. Retrieved from www.businessinsider.com/these-6-corporations-control-90-of-the-media-in-america-2012-6

DON'T GET LEFT BEHIND

By Axel Sippach

Someone once said that the only thing constant is change. We are living in the fastest-moving and changing times of human history. Twentieth-century visionary and inventor, Buckminster Fuller, discovered that, until 1900, human knowledge had doubled approximately every century, but, by the end of World War II, knowledge was doubling every 25 years or so. Today on average, human knowledge is doubling every 13 months, and according to IBM, the building out of the internet will eventually lead to the doubling of knowledge every 12 hours. You cannot resist change. And how we communicate, for better or worse, is also changing rapidly.

Whether you are building a ministry, non-profit, movement, or business, you cannot afford to ignore this exponentially-growing phenomenon of the past 15-20 years on the Mountain of Media—Social Media. Should you chose to ignore the changes, claiming you're just too "old school" to change, well, prepare to get seriously left behind, remaining stuck in the previous century.

Three major game-changers over the past two decades that have created much change in how we communicate are: the internet, the mobile phone, and social media. About 80% or more of the world is doing social media now via their phone vs. laptop. And most Millennials now get their news from Social Media vs. Cable News outlets. It's a new day. Twitter has over 330 million users, Instagram has over 800 million, and Facebook now has over 2 billion as of this writing. There are over 1 billion YouTube users, with over 5 billion videos seen every day. We better get with the program, understand the times, figure it out and seize the moment, or get left behind in the dust.

Prophetic Forecasting

1 Chronicles 12:32 speaks of the sons of the tribe of Issachar having understanding of the times and knowing what Israel should do. This is speaking of prophetic insight—understanding what's happening now, prophetically seeing the future, and then having the spiritual wisdom to know how to navigate the current times accurately, making the right choices that produce future results. This must be how we operate if we are to scale and influence the mountains of culture. It seems as if the Church at large is always behind the times, struggling to catch up, instead of being on the prophetic cutting edge and helping lead change in every generation. We have to start doing better. And many Millennial leaders are leading the way. That's how they're wired.

Social Media is defined by the Merriam Webster online dictionary as: "forms of electronic communication (such as websites for social networking and micro-blogging) through which users create online communities to share information, ideas, personal messages, and other content (such as videos)." It is a powerful tool of communication, used by many Jesus followers now, to influence the world for the Kingdom of God, but also used by dark, sinister, demonic forces for all kinds of ungodly purposes, including recruiting and radicalizing young people through varying ideologies to commit acts of terrorism.

Christians must increase their Kingdom footprint of influence and leverage the power of this critical part of the Mountain of Media, in order to have a fighting chance to win the culture wars currently raging in society for the minds of the next generation.

Social Media has leveled the playing, where everyone can now have a voice at very little cost. An idea can travel the globe in seconds and reach millions. What will you do with that voice? What is your voice? What is your message? How can you be the light of the world and the salt of the Earth on social media? How are you building your platform of influence? You now have the opportunity to not only post written content, but also videos, with Facebook Live and Periscope in heated competition for dominance. You can have your own internet TV channel right on your

Facebook page for free. For just a few dollars, you can build a sharp, inexpensive website as a blog to create videos and content. You can build a YouTube channel for free.

You Have a Voice—Use it!

You have a voice. Now you must discover how to have it stand out from all the other "noise" out there. This is very critical, whether you are a Christian building a ministry, church, non-profit, movement, or business. You will not have success in scaling the other mountains without media, and today, most importantly, Social Media. Who are you? What is your message? Why does the world need to hear it? Why do they need to connect with you? How does what you carry add value to their lives? What *good news* do you have to bring to this mountain? How can you build an online community of like-minded people that want to be change agents, influencing the culture for Jesus Christ?

While some individual believers may have a *special call* to Social Media and the Mountain of Media as a whole, I believe all of God's people are to utilize this platform of influence. We have seen videos of grandmas in their 80's and 90's go viral on Facebook, touching the hearts of millions. So please don't tell me you're too old. Edythe Kirchmaier got her first computer at age 95, signed up for Facebook at 105, and grew the page to over 55,000 followers who adored her until she passed away at 107. Listen—age is just a number. Stop making excuses. Just stop it. It's time for action. Just do it!

Satan is looking to dominate this new Social Media phenomenon as another tool of his "mind control" strategies to shape the next generation. Jesus said in Mathew chapter 16 that He was building His Church right at the very gates of hell. The Church is not to be in a defensive posture. Satan is to be in a defensive posture, because the Church is on the offensive, advancing the Kingdom of Light into the darkness. We must bring good news and speak truth to Social Media through inspired and revelatory content. We must be anointed **thought-leaders** and **problem-solvers** whose social media content stands out to capture the attention of the masses.

The Apostle Paul says in Colossians 2:2-3 that in Christ are hidden all the treasures of wisdom and knowledge, and his purpose was to encourage the believers to have the full riches of complete understanding regarding this mystery. If those treasures are in Christ, and Christ by His Spirit is in us, then those treasures of wisdom and knowledge are also in us, ready to be mined and manifested by the Spirit. Destiny is in you. You have received the high calling of God in Christ Jesus, which I believe is "sonship." Jesus came to bring many sons to glory. He wants you to live a life of Kingdom purpose, whether that is ministry in the Church or in the marketplace. You are living epistles, written not with ink, but by the Spirit of God. He has given you a voice. He has given you a message which is "good news." And you are the messenger whose anointed feet are beautiful to scale mountains and say to Zion, "Your God reigns" (Isaiah 52:7).

How Do I Get Started?

Before discussing the technical aspects of building Social Media platforms, here are three questions you need to answer: (1) Why? (2) What? (3) How?

You can't really figure out well **what** to do, or **how** you're going to do it until you answer **why** you want to do it. I think your *why* is at least 50% of the equation here. Knowing your *why* is what will get you out of bed in the morning. It's what creates energy regarding the things you're passionate about. Why do you want to do this—build a Social Media platform? Your "Why" may have to do with the message that has been marinating in your spirit for some time, ready to be proclaimed. Your "Why" is your cause. What are you passionate about? What are your gifts and talents? What are the deep desires in your heart that God has put there? What is your purpose? What is your mission? What is your "Why?" "Why" do you want to take this mountain?

Once you begin to understand that, now you can begin to tackle your "What" and "How." "What" am I going to do? "How" am I going to do it? What Social Media platform(s) will work best for my "Why" and "What" am I going to do with it? And then "How" do I begin? What are my next steps? "How" do I build this thing? Your "Why" is more the "spiritual" side, and your "What" and "How" are more the practical side.

Research & Development

You will have to put the time in to research your best options of where to start: Twitter (Periscope), Facebook (FB Live), Instagram, Snapchat, YouTube, Website/blog, etc. There are so many books out there on Amazon.com you can find, along with so many free resources in the way of articles on Google and informational videos on YouTube. At the moment, I am personally primarily using Facebook and Facebook Live, along with a website. I have both a Facebook personal page with about 14,000 friends and followers, and a fan page with about 54,000 followers at the time of this writing that has been built over the past four years. I do most of my posting on that page now. I also have an Instagram page I recently started. Let me focus the rest of this chapter on some tips on building your Facebook presence.

Many of you reading this are on Facebook already, so I won't get into the details of how to start. What you mainly have to decide is if you prefer to just have a personal page or also build what before was call a fan page. Facebook is constantly changing the rules and also their algorithm formula which determines which of your friends or followers can see your posts in their newsfeed. Don't read any books or articles to learn things about Facebook that are older than a year or two. They will already be outdated.

Personal pages have limitations, such as not being able to do a paid boost on posts. Fan pages will take a lot more effort to build and get the same response you have been getting on your personal one, but in the long run, will pay off much more if you invest the time and energy into it. My fan page four years ago was just sitting there with very little action and about 3,000 Likes. I made a concerted effort every day to build it. Now, four years later, it's close to 54,000 Likes. And I'm on my way to reach 100,000 soon. But it takes work, and a lot of experimentation at first with trial and error to see what does or doesn't work on your page. And much of this focus will also have to do with the type of audience you are trying to build.

Here are some tips I can give you to help build your Facebook page:

1. **Authentic**: If people meet you in person, is it a reflection of what they thought you would be like from your page? Or will they get a big shock? Don't be doing photo ops with expensive luxury cars, when you actually roll up in a raggedy old beater. Don't use photos of yourself from 10 and 20 years ago, so then people actually meet you in person and wonder if you got hit by the ugly bus. Nothing wrong with a little photo editing on current pics to bring out the best you, but don't overdo it to the place of where it is just fake and you've airbrushed away every slightest wrinkle. Be real. Does your personality—and also spirituality—on Facebook match what people will experience in person? Bottom line—be authentic. Don't just copycat what someone else is doing on Facebook. Others can inspire you; but remember, it's all about your "Why." Why do you want to do this? Your "Why" becomes part of your authentic you. Let it reflect on Facebook.

2. **Experiment**: You will have to try different types of posts, including lengths of posts to see what your audience is interested in. I use short, inspirational posts which can have more traction as far as FB likes go. But I also use longer, teaching-type posts because I want to give greater value and substance. They usually don't get as much traction as far as Likes do, but they help establish my authority in the field that I am writing about. It's all about adding value to people's lives. Occasionally, I post pics of my life, my travels, and ministry to bring people closer and build more relationships with my audience. Occasionally, I will touch on controversial subjects that I feel very passionately about such as injustice, but try to also do it with a lot of wisdom. So experiment. See what works for you. The more likes, shares, and comments on posts, the more the algorithm formula will favor your posts in the newsfeed of followers and fans. Post daily. You can also schedule posts for a week or more out. You have to be consistent. Take it seriously.

3. **Facebook Live:** Facebook is looking to dominate in the area of videos and the more you go Live, the more it will show in the newsfeeds of followers. Make sure you have good content and a good presentation. I am appalled by some of the Live broadcasts I see. Sometimes the content may be fine, but the presentation is atrocious.

Write out some points for your Live, even if you plan to flow. Let people know at the beginning what topic you will be covering. Make sure you have great natural outside or supplemented inside lighting so your face is bright. If you use your laptop, consider investing in an auxiliary USB Logitech Webcam like the 4K Brio for under $200. Otherwise, make sure your phone does a good job with its camera, and have your phone on a mini tripod to stabilize it. When you have completed a Live, go over and evaluate it. How was your content, presentation, audio, lighting, etc.? How was the response? What could you do better? Experiment with doing a Live at different times during the day. See what the best time is for your audience. This is like having your own TV channel for the world. This is an amazing platform for your voice—your message. Will you be a good steward of it?

4. **Just Do It:** Someone once said, "Beginning is half done." You just have to start. Make a plan and work the plan. Remember, you have a voice. And now you have been given an amazing, new and free tool of communication called Social Media to reach the world with your message. Whether you are building a ministry, non-profit, movement, or scaling the Mountain of Business, you cannot afford to ignore Social Media. If you are running for public office on the Mountain of Government, you cannot ignore Social Media. If you want to reform the Mountain of Education, you cannot ignore Social Media. If you are looking to gain influence on the Mountain of Arts & Entertainment, you cannot ignore Social Media. Those on any of the other mountains of influence will at some level have to connect with the Mountain of Media, and specifically with Social Media, to have an impact on this generation, and generations to come. You can't afford to wait. This is your time. Your voice is needed. What are you waiting for? Go scale this mountain!

Apostolic Prayer:

Father, I pray in Jesus' Name that your sons and daughters would awaken to the urgency of the hour, that you would speak to them regarding involvement on this Mountain of Social Media, so their voice might be heard, and the revelation in their spirit might go forth to the ends of the

Earth. Lord, you said in Psalms 19:4 (ESV) *"Their voice goes out through all the Earth and their words to the end of the world. In them he has set a tent for the sun."* Father, let them realize that their spirit is like a tabernacle, filled with revelation that you have given them in order to shine like the sun in all its brilliance. May they pen words of wisdom to reach a generation. As written in Psalm 45:1, may their hearts be stirred by noble themes, and may their tongue be like the pen of a ready, skillful writer. I pray that you will give them a scribe's anointing to write and post on Social Media with words of instruction, inspiration, motivation, wisdom, and revelation. May they truly realize they are carriers of "good news" as their beautiful feet scale this mountain of influence. May they see the lives of many touched and transformed through their posts as their voice is heard on this mountain. And may your favor shine upon them as they "go," sent with your apostolic anointing and thrust to reclaim the Mountain of Social Media.

Prophetic Decrees:

I decree that believers will find their voice in the midst of all the noise, and understand with greater clarity their purpose, mission, and message. With courage and boldness, let them scale this Mountain of Social Media and bring the light of truth to dispel the darkness.

I decree that the Mountain of the Lord's Temple (Isaiah 2:2) will be established as the highest ruler of all the other mountains, including the Mountain of Social Media, and that all nations will flow to it.

I decree that, as the Kingdom influence of God's people grows on the Mountain of Social Media, many people will have a hunger to say, "come let us go up to the Mountain of the Lord" (Isaiah 2:3).

I decree that the Word of the Lord will come forth from Zion, from the people of God influencing Social Media, and they will teach His ways so that the nations might walk in His paths (Isaiah 2:3).

I decree that the settling of conflicts with the aim of bringing peace will take place through God's anointed "social entrepreneurs" gaining more and more influence on Social Media Mountain, thus resulting in swords beaten into plowshares and spears into pruning hooks, so nations will not take up swords against nations (Isaiah 2:4).

I decree that you will walk in the light of the present truth revelation as it relates to the Seven Mountains of Culture, and that you will "arise and shine for your light has come," because the glory of the Lord has risen upon you (Isaiah 2:5; 60:1).

I decree that the voice of God's people and the words, the message they carry, will extend to the ends of the Earth through Social Media, and that God's Word they proclaim will not return void, but will accomplish His desire and purpose for which it is sent (Psalm 19:4; Isaiah 55:11).

GLOBAL MEDIA:
Influencing Today's Culture and Fulfilling Biblical Prophecy

By Cherie Banks

Global media is a new world superpower affecting your daily life in unimaginable ways. Modern living powers up digital devices and plugs into augmented realities. While technological advancements are convenient, there is a cost. Global media gives you on-demand broadcasting to everything, everywhere, for everyone's consumption. It controls what you see and hear on television, radio, music, movies, videos, podcasts, software, and the Internet. Global media is a subtle, yet powerful force shaping your worldview by programming your thoughts, decisions, and actions. This superpower identifies who you are in a culturally-diverse universe and can influence up to 7.6 billion people in an instant to sway the popular opinion of the planet's inhabitants.

Imagine if you could influence humans all over the world by controlling the terminology, timing, and transmission of information delivered every second of the day. You would have the power to manipulate the cultural configuration and idiosyncratic identity of billions of people. It would grant you domination in any sphere of society solely for your best interests. That is a remarkable thought, but in fact, a realism for global media giants.

In June 2017, The Guardian, which covers American and international news for an online, global audience, reported studies from the University of Oxford that propaganda on social media is used to manipulate worldwide public opinion. The Oxford Internet Institute's Computational Propaganda Research Project produced a nine-country study including the United States of America, finding widespread use of social media for promoting lies, misinformation, and propaganda by governments and individuals.

Professor of Internet Studies at Oxford, Philip Howard said that "the lies, the junk, the misinformation" of traditional propaganda is widespread online and "supported by Facebook or Twitter's algorithms." These case studies found that global media is knowingly and willfully broadcasting untruthful and inaccurate information. In the New Testament, Apostle Paul warns not to be deceived, deluded or misled (Galatians 6:7 AMP). The Old Testament states that God's people are destroyed for lack of knowledge (Hosea 4:6 NIV). Therefore, it is imperative to know the truth and discern deceptive practices. Today, there is an unprecedented urgency for Christians to change the corrupt culture of global media by transforming it with truth and accuracy in an ever-evolving millennial marketplace. This reading summons you to speak, act, and move the global media mountain for such a time as this! Your commitment to living God's Word online as well as offline is critical for Christianity.

It's not surprising that global media reigns at the summit of the media mountain. It encompasses every form of media with the greatest population reach on the planet. TechCrunch's statistics (June 2017) reported that Facebook is the largest social app, with 2 billion users, compared to YouTube's 1.5 billion, WeChat's 889 million, Instagram's 700+ million, Twitter's 328 million, and Snapchat's estimated 255 million. Beyond YouTube, only Facebook's other apps have more than 1 billion, including WhatsApp and Facebook Messenger, with 1.2 billion each. The current state of global media is crying out for Christians to implement cultural change against expansive world corruption. Otherwise, this superpower will increase its influence in pursuit of its own purposes in a split nanosecond.

Global media is not evil *per se*. It depends on how it's being used, by whom, and for what reason. Unfortunately, trending lifestyles are driven by big data and mass media. Global media has mastered customizing your pre-packaged persona for its specific purposes. It precisely programs your life for geo-targeting campaigns to promote agendas, produce profits, and progress powers. However, this is not the only power with a purpose concerning you. God is also working to fulfill His good purpose in you (Philippians 2:13 NIV). Global media (*the world's leading superpower*) and God (*the highest supernatural power*) have intended purposes for you. The good news is that you have your own willpower to decide which purpose you want fulfilled in your life and on the Earth. Choose to change the culture of global media by influencing its meaning, movement, and message with God's Word.

Despite the findings of global media's unscrupulous functionality, it can be transfigured to serve worthy life-giving and soul-saving purposes instead. This calls upon Christians to rise up in transforming the integrity and character of this superpower in scriptural alignment. This starts with you, here and now. The Bible instructs to eagerly pursue harmony for the edification and development of one another (Romans 14:19 AMPC). This means that God created you to be an influencer. You have power and authority to possess the Media Mountain doing God's greatest good. As a Christian, you are responsible and accountable to influence people with His precepts. For example, you can write Christ-centered content, produce work inspired by the Holy Spirit, create systems based on Scriptures, broadcast narratives to birth new life, code programs/apps that encrypt the heart of God, or execute business strategies derived from divine wisdom and revelation. Of course, there are so many more things you can do!

The most fascinating purpose of global media is the compelling earmarks of fulfilling biblical prophecy. This superpower shows a supernatural sign in preparing the way for Jesus Christ's return. The twenty-first century is the Information Age, which is exploding with increased knowledge at insurmountable speed. This was foretold by God's prophet, Daniel. The Lord told him to "shut up the words and seal the book, even to the time of the end as many shall run to and fro, and knowledge shall be increased" (Daniel 12:4 KJV). Daniel didn't understand this since he lived in an ancient world when knowledge was an extremely scarce and rare commodity. However, in the modern world, this increased knowledge perfectly fits the age and time you are living in today.

A brief fact-check of Daniel's prophecy is confirmed. The Industry Tap reported that the accumulation of knowledge doubles every 12 months, soon to be every 12 hours. This was premised upon Buckminster Fuller's *"Knowledge Doubling Curve."* Until 1900, human knowledge doubled approximately every century. By the end of World War II, knowledge was doubling every 25 years. Industry Tap points out that nowadays different types of knowledge have different rates of growth. Nanotechnology is doubling every two years and clinical knowledge every 18 months; but on average, human knowledge is doubling every 13 months. According to IBM, the build-out of the "internet of things" will lead to the doubling of knowledge every 12 hours.

Another biblical prophecy on global media is in the book of Revelation. St. John reveals that people of every tribe, language, and nation will witness the persecution and murder of God's two prophets in Jerusalem by the beast (Revelation 11:1-14). This live broadcast of killings before the entire world describes the revolutionary technology of global media. The prophecy also predicts that the world will continue to watch as these deaths will be publicly celebrated for three and a half days (Revelation, *id*). Here, St. John gives a glimpse into the futuristic live streaming of horrific murders for every nation to view simultaneously. Global media is rapidly revealing the mysteries of these biblical prophecies, thus signifying the last days.

Unfortunately, you are gaining greater access to watching bone-chilling murders occur in real-time via global media. Gruesome, graphic live images of people being killed are in your everyday news feed or push notification within the blink of an eye. The Bible says, "The struggle is not against flesh and blood, but against the rulers, against the authorities, against the powers of this dark world and against the spiritual forces of evil in the heavenly realms" (Ephesians 6:12 NIV). You cannot deny that global media has become a digital display for the devil's handiwork. In order to overthrow such dark powers and evil forces from the world's demonic programming, Christians must go to the top of the media mountain and transform it into God's truth, hope, and love for humanity. I pray that you will speak boldly, act courageously, and move this mighty mountain!

Prayer Points

1. I exhibit Christ-like character in every medium of global media including my work and personal life. I represent love, joy, peace, patience, kindness, goodness, faithfulness, gentleness, and self-control (Galatians 5:22-23).
2. I reject all shameful deeds and underhanded methods for worldly deception, collective, or individual interests and I do not trick anyone with false or inaccurate information (2 Corinthians 4:1-2).
3. I have biblical integrity, pure intentions, and righteous footprints in the digital world and in all the Earth (Proverbs 2:20-21).
4. I speak the truth in love and diligently convey the Word of God on social platforms and private interactions growing more like Christ in every way (Ephesians 4:15, 2 Timothy 2:15).
5. I live a godly life both online and offline, producing good fruit and in giving my gifts of the Spirit (Galatians 5:22-23, 1 Corinthians 12:8-10).

Declaration

I am a Kingdom influencer, well-equipped to transform the global media mountain with God's power and authority. I serve as the Lord's instrument of influence over billions of people online and offline. I edify and exhort people around the world with God's Word. I am zealous and courageous to do God's work fearing no one, but the Lord. I am created to change cultural influences, cast down worldly systems, and build up God's people. I raise my voice in various forms of media contributing my gifts and talents in accordance with God's assignment for my life. I will not allow global media to program my life. I refuse and reject deceptive practices and world corruption. I walk in truth, righteousness, and biblical teaching. I use my words, writing, content, conversation, creativity, intellect, knowledge, professional opportunities, and personal experiences to speak life, healing, restoration, love, peace, and blessings to every person and all nations. I live in the ways of Jesus Christ and exemplify a lifestyle that is pleasing to God. I am responsible and accountable to report accurate and truthful information. I pray and protect my unsaved brothers and sisters and fellow Christians from dark powers and evil forces designed to destroy their divine destiny. I decree the world will witness my uprising in Christ by changing the cultural climate of global media and moving the media mountain for God's glory!

---

[1] Hern, A. (2017, June). Facebook and Twitter are being used to manipulate public opinion - report. The Guardian. Retrieved from https://www.theguardian.com/technology/2017/jun/19/social-media-proganda-manipulating-public-opinion-bots-accounts-facebook-twitter

[2] Constine, J. (2017, June). Facebook now has 2 billion monthly users...and responsibility. TechCrunch. Retrieved from https://techcrunch.com/2017/06/27/facebook-2-billion-users/

[3] Russell Schilling, D. (April 2013). Knowledge doubling every 12 months, soon to be every 12 hours. Industry Tap. Retrieved from http://www.industrytap.com/knowledge-doubling-every-12-months-soon-to-be-every-12-hours/3950

WHO IS SHAPING WHO?
HOW MEDIA INFLUENCES THE MASSES

By Alexander Gray

"And be not conformed to this world: but be ye transformed by the renewing of your mind, that ye may prove what is that good, and acceptable, and perfect, will of God." Romans 12:2 (KJV)

Definition and Intent

Media as defined by Dictionary.com is 1: The main means of mass communication; 2. The plural form of medium- which is defined as - The intervening substance through which impressions are conveyed to the senses; 3. The substance in which an organism lives or is cultivated.

In order to begin to understand the influence of media and why it is a mountain to be dealt with, we must first focus on sound; specifically, the spoken word. Let us look at the word *speak*, which means "to give voice to, utter words, or articulate sounds with the ordinary voice" (Dictionary.com). Words have the power to decree and bring about change. Change can either be for good or bad. The kind of spirit behind the spoken word, is what gives it power.

In Genesis, God spoke what He wanted into existence: *"And God said, let there be light: and there was light" Gen. 1:3 (KJV).* God spoke to the earth (ground), then vegetation, animals, and life appeared. He spoke to the heavens, and birds became. With His words, things were created, things changed from one form to the next and order was again set in place. Media is an entity that influences and cultivates impressions within the senses and mindsets of people. It shapes thinking, decision-making, and moral standards through sound and sight.

The images that we see over the airwaves are not the right images before the people. In the online article "How the Media Molds the World" from *Tomorrow's World* (author Douglas Winnail), it is stated that, "Television, movies and the internet are having an effect on mankind that would have been unimaginable even a century ago. The media—print and electronic— shape our lives and our minds in ways that most fail to realize, and with sobering effects."

According to Pediatrics Child Health, media has a profound influence on the psychosocial development of children (Impact of Media Use on Children and Youth, 2003). A national survey in the U.S. found that children aged 8 to 18 years have an average media usage time of 7 hours and 38 minutes. The longer the viewing time, the more of an impact and influence television has upon the child. The adverse result is that the world on television becomes the real world. According to the American Academy of Pediatrics, "Exposure to violence in media, including television, movies, music, and video games represents a significant risk to the health of children and adolescents. Extensive research evidence indicates that media violence can contribute to aggressive behavior, desensitization to violence, and fear of being harmed" (Impact of Media Use on Children and Youth, 2003). Research shows that young people view an average of 10,000 acts of violence per year with 61% of the shows containing violence. Media is also a contributing factor to early sexual initiation, promiscuity, the risk of obesity, and other behavioral problems (J. Indian Assoc. Child Adolesc. Mental Health, 2012).

Sight and Sound Go Hand In Hand

Sound plays an important role in the lives of people. It can cause a person to either react or respond depending upon what feeling is produced from the sound that was released. The Word says: "*[24] And he said unto them, Take heed what ye hear: with what measure ye mete, it shall be measured to you: and unto you that hear shall more be given" Mark 4:24 (KJV)*. God instructs us to be mindful of what we hear because whatever we give our mind to will become part of our being. Sound and images go hand in hand. The word states very simply, *"Eat thou not the bread of him that hath and evil eye, neither desire thou his dainty meats: For as he thinketh in his heart, so is he: Eat and drink, saith he to thee; but his heart is not with thee"* Proverbs 23:6-7(KJV).

Thinking is the process of thought based on what you feed your mind daily. What you see or hear determines your memories and experiences. Thinking is the process that allows a person to analyze what they see or hear, and then create beliefs and actions. This is why a person must mind their eye gates. *Luke 11:34(KJV) states, [34] "The light of the body is the eye: therefore when thine eye is single, thy whole body also is full of light; but when thine eye is evil, thy body also is full of darkness."* This line of scripture sums up why the Media is such a powerful influencer to the development of a nation, a world, or a people, be it to its advancement or detriment.

Marketers and advertisers use the science behind media by manipulating senses, emotions, and feelings through the sounds and images they produce, thus leading the masses to adapt their mindsets, culture, and standards to the "trends" of the world. Through subliminal messages, one can change what is now considered **acceptable**. We see examples of this every day; look at things or ideas that are acceptable in today's society or those that are not in the last 10 to 15 years.

In 2001, if you were to watch or listen to any form of media, there was still a level of moral fiber, or standard that was being shown. You would see a lesson, a clear delineation of right and wrong, where the idea of God was something that was demonstrated in daily interactions. Even in the music industry, there was a message to enlighten, empower, educate, or just have fun. Then the switch happened. It began subtly in the intervening substance or spirit and began to project or promote political correctness and new age thinking. The focus shifted to monetary success, possessions, and status. There was a shift to a feel-good message. This change did not happen overnight, but it was systematic and strategic through subliminal messaging and marketing.

We Wrestle Not After Flesh and Blood

What is this intervening substance called **media**? It is a spirit, but whose spirit is it? It is an intervening substance, which means it is in between two things—positive and negative, good and evil. We see in Genesis how God used His sound, His voice, to speak life into existence and set things in order in their proper place. What sound is setting things in motion in the world now? It is not a sound of order; it is a sound of the seven deadly sins: envy, gluttony, greed, lust, pride, sloth, and wrath. The word says in 1 Corinthians 14:33 (KJV), *"For God is not the author of confusion, but of peace, as in all churches of the saints."* So, who is the author of this confusion?

In Ephesians 2:1-2 (KJV), Apostle Paul states, *"And you hath he quickened, who were dead in trespasses and sins; Wherein in time past ye walked according to the course of this world, according to the prince of the power of the air, the spirit that now worketh in the children of disobedience:"* The "prince" that Apostle Paul is referring to is Satan and he has genuine power over the world *(1 John 5:19 and Luke 4:6)*, its systems, and the airwaves. Though he has this power or authority, it is limited and subject to the sovereign power of God. We have to take back this mountain and undo the misdirection of our generation, and change the focus from the world's agenda and place it back on the right order of the Kingdom of God.

The question is, how do we begin? Remember, Ephesians 6:12 (KJV) tells us, *"For we wrestle not against flesh and blood, but against principalities, against powers, against the rulers of the darkness of this world, against spiritual wickedness in high places."* God spoke the change He wanted to see and John 6:63 (KJV) says, *"It is the spirit that quickeneth; the flesh profiteth nothing: the words that I speak unto you, they are spirit, and they are life."* Take back the mountain of "Media" by speaking and casting out the spirit of demonic influence that is corrupting it. [23] *"For verily I say unto you, That whosoever shall say unto this mountain, Be thou removed, and be thou cast into the sea; and shall not doubt in his heart, but shall believe that those things which he saith shall come to pass; he shall have whatsoever he saith"* Mark 11:23 (KJV).

God reminds us to be mindful of our hearing. *(Mark 4:24)*
God reminds us that we have been set apart. *(1 Peter 2:9)*

God reminds us to be mindful of the path we choose. (*2 Timothy 2:22*)

With these tools, we should be doing what the Apostles of old and Daniel did *(Acts 17: 6, Daniel 1:8 & Daniel 6:26)*. We are the atmosphere-shifters, carriers of God's presence, so we should be changing the world; not the world molding and shaping us.

Prayer Points

1. We take authority over the prince and the power of the air - *Ephesians 2:2 (KJV)*
2. We bind the strongman over the media and we spoil his goods and loose him from his assignment - *Matthew 12:29 (KJV)*
3. We pray that the effectual fervent prayer takes back the media in the name of Jesus - *James 5:16 (KJV)*
4. We release the angels to dismantle negative communication that is being infiltrated by the media - *Psalms 103:20 (KJV)*
5. We decree and declare that the voice of the Lord shall be heard through the Media *Job 22: 28 (KJV)*
6. We take authority over the princes and the governors that rule the media and we command them to cease and desist - *Daniel 3:3 (KJV)*
7. We decree and declare that the false idols that are erected in the Media shall be dismantled in the name of Jesus - *Psalms 115: 4-9 (KJV)*
8. We pray in the name of Jesus that the Lord will open the eyes of His people to see the order that He has for the Media - *2Kings 6:17 (KJV)*
9. We decree and declare that the heathen will submit to the will of the Lord – *Psalms 2:8 (KJV)*
10. Lord, we thank you that you teach our hands to war against the god over the media and pull down his negative influence over the people - *Psalms 144:1-2 (KJV)*

---

[1] (n.d.). Retrieved from Dictionary.com: https://www.dictionary.com

[2] *Impact of Media Use on Children and Youth.* (2003, May-June-). Retrieved from Paediatrics Child Health- Canadian Paediatric Society: htips://www.ncbi.n/m.nih.gov/pmc/articles

[3] J. Indian Assoc. Child Adolesc. Mental Health. (2012). *Harmful Effects of Media on Children and Adolescents.*

[4] Winnail, D. S. (2003, January- February). "*How The Media Molds The World.* Retrieved from Tomorrow's World: https://www.tomorrowsworld.org/magazines/2003

CHAPTER 3

THE MOUNTAIN OF EDUCATION

Our educational system in America and many other countries is in trouble. Even on the U.S Department of Education and individual state websites, you will see that the main topic of discussion is reform. Our public educational system is failing our students and in need of major updating and reformation. What that looks like is being passionately debated from different perspectives. This is a time that Christian teachers and administrators called to this mountain must understand the mind of Christ for this generation and offer creative and innovative solutions to the plethora of problems that exist. This is one of the reasons that private Christian and charter schools are doing so well. Many are able to implement different experimental and innovative approaches to education that are having powerful measurable results, along with the opportunity afforded by Private Christian schools to teach from a biblical worldview.

The Mountain of Education is one of the primary mind-molders of culture as it shapes the thinking of the next generation. If parents on the Family Mountain are not discipling their children according to the ways of the Lord, then they are abdicating their responsibilities by relegating this task to, in many cases, a public school system promoting secular humanism and situational ethics. Someone is disciplining your impressionable children and shaping their minds. If it's not happening at home, it will happen at school. This mountain must be reclaimed for future generations through anointed and passionate teachers and administrators who will become voices for change. Some will take on the current public school system to bring major reformation from within. And others will pioneer new experimental and innovative private schools that will much more quickly produce greater results in shaping the hearts and minds of students.

SCHOOL-TO-PRISON PIPELINE

By Donita Gordon, Ed. S

God has giving us the power and authority to grab the mountain of education by the horns and command it to line up with His will upon the Earth. After working as a teacher with young adults in an incarcerated environment for several years, I have had the opportunity to listen to various testimonies of how our youth started on a downward spiral into a life of imprisonment. Many of the students indicated it resulted from behavioral infractions as far back as elementary school. Numerous teachers, staff, and administrators have exhausted themselves trying to decrease the number of behavioral and security concerns.

Governing authorities have held on to 1980's zero-tolerance policies to reduce the number of behavioral occurrences. Steven Teske has defined the phrase *zero-tolerance* as a policy that mandates the application of a predetermined consequence, most often severe, and punitive in nature, regardless of the seriousness of behavior, mitigating circumstances, or situational context (Teske, 2014). A student in Virginia was cuffed and suspended after accusations of stealing a 65-cent carton of milk during lunch while approved for the Free Lunch program (NG, Alfred, 2016). This policy has limited the amount of positive behavioral interventions, increased the number of referrals to the criminal justice system, and increased the out of school suspension time amongst students. This type of strain on the school climate creates an educational storm within the schools, courtrooms, and communities. 'The practice of pushing kids out of school and toward the juvenile and criminal justice systems has become known as the "school-to-prison pipeline"' (National Education Association members, 2013).

Many policies have proven to favor incarceration with our youth. The favorable actions include long-term suspensions, referrals, and on-school restraints (Ferriss, 2014). "Perhaps the most disturbing finding is that nationally, on average, 36 percent of black male students with disabilities enrolled in middle and high schools were suspended at least once in 2009-2010" (Ferriss, 2014). In 2010, more than 3 million students were suspended from school. The data also showed African-American students are suspended and expelled at a rate three times greater than white students and accounted for 70 percent of the referrals to the police (National Education Association members, 2013).

Studies have also proved in recent years how schools have increased knowledge of the practices and offered wrap-around services for at-risk youth. School divisions have implemented best practices for behavior modification and new strategies to support the educational, social, emotional, and physical wellbeing of the student. Numerous stakeholders are committed to improving the climate, diverting students away from the school-to-prison pipeline.

Members of the body of Christ must take a strong stance not only in the areas of academics but also in helping to interrupt the pipeline. It is imperative to have dedicated community liaisons established to foster the "It takes a Village" African Proverb. This viewpoint will help to inaugurate community connections with schools, law enforcement officers, and community agencies where warranted. Parents, guardians, teachers, coaches, and persons of faith must continue to teach and train up youth with the Word of God. Timothy is a great example of how teaching our youth the Word of God can foster a godly relationship and steer kids away from trouble (2 Timothy 1:5). Timothy's faith in God is traced from his grandmother Lois, through his mother Eunice. This represents a strong generation of faith for Timothy. This great example of training a child in the way he should go offers a commitment of hope for both unbelieving and believing youth.

Another great biblical example is found in the book of 1 Samuel 2:24-34. While Eli was concerned about the transgressions his sons committed against the Law of Moses, he was guilty of neglecting his governing responsibilities towards them. Many may choose to focus on the terror Eli's sons were committing but we must take a closer look at Eli himself, as a teacher of influence. Eli spent much time instructing Samuel on the biblical teachings. He taught Samuel how to hear and obey the Voice of God (1 Samuel 3:10). Unfortunately, Eli neglected to guide his own sons on hearing and obeying the Voice of God.

Lastly, you can find a practical example of how to get involved using the *Church Adopt a School Organization* founded by Dr. Tony Evans. This vision emerged over 30 years ago, when a principal at a local high school wanted a resolution to the gang activity and other disruptive behaviors within the school building. Dr. Evans answered the call by sending 12 men to walk the halls and help restore order within the institute. This powerful vision helped to not only restore order, but also built a connection that would interrupt the school-to-prison pipeline.

Often times, we have many responsibilities and assignments which may captivate our time. It is imperative that the Church refuses to ignore the responsibilities to rear young men and women within the local schools, churches, neighboring communities, and homes. We must take back the governing authority of our families, cities, and schools and rear our youth in the admonition of the Lord. "And, ye fathers, provoke not your children to wrath: but bring them up in the nurture and admonition of the Lord" (Ephesians 6:4).

Prayer

Heavenly Father, we acknowledge you in all of our ways as our personal Lord and Savior Jesus Christ. We ask you to forgive us of the sins we have committed along with the sins of our fathers. We invite your presence back into our schools. We bind the spirit of rebellion, refusal of obedience or order, and open resistance against order in the Name of Jesus Christ. We release a spirit of truth, obedience to authority, and peace into public and private schools (1 Sam 15:23, Luke 4:6, Psalm 51:10). We bind the spirit of defiance that comes to challenge, and proudly refuse to obey authority, those who are told to obey and they immediately do the opposite. In the name of Jesus Christ, we release a spirit of truth, humility, contrite spirit, and submissiveness to authority within the schools

Psalms 32:9, Proverbs 6:16-19 - We bind the spirit of rejection, dismissing or refusing the order of Authority, in the name of Jesus Christ. We release a spirit of adoption and love into the minds, bodies, souls, and spirits of our youth (Mark 6:4, Romans 8:15). Father, bless and cover the students, teachers, staff, administration, and governing boards. In Jesus' name, we pray. Amen.

Affirmation

The Lord will establish our youth as a holy people, as He promised, if they keep the commands of the Lord their God and walk in obedience to Him (Deuteronomy 28: 1-9)

---

[1] "Home." *Adopt a School Initiative*. Web. Retrieved 07 Oct. 2017.

[2] Ferriss, Susan. "New Report Highlights Disproportionate School Discipline for Minorities: School Suspensions Put Kids at Risk for Dropping out or Worse." 19 May 2014: Web. Oct.-Nov. 2017.

[3] Ng, Alfred. "Va. Student Arrested after Accused of Stealing Free Milk at Lunch." *NY Daily News*. NEW YORK DAILY NEWS, 24 May 2016. Web. 07 Oct. 2017.

[4] Teske, Steve. "A Study of Zero Tolerance Policies in Schools" A Multi-integrated Systems Approach to Improve Outcomes for Adolescents." *Journal of Child and Adolescent Psychiatric Nursing"* (2014): Web.

[5] "The School-to-Prison Pipeline: Time to Shut It Down." *NEA Today*. N.p., 12 Sept. 2016. Web. 07 Oct. 2017.

SEPARATION OF CHURCH AND STATE: BRIDGING THE GAP

By Tressena Jones

The Heart of the Matter

According to the National Center for Education Statistics, about 50.7 million students started school in the fall of 2017, and 3.2 million teachers also started school at the same time as employees in the public school system. When you look at those numbers, I hope that you can see what sometimes gets lost when we look at statistical data, the people. Those numbers should bring a perspective of how many people are being touched just by sending kids to school every day.

Many have heard the saying that children are our future. As a matter of fact, a very popular song says, "the children are our future, teach them well and let them lead the way. Show them all the beauty they possess inside." The truth is, children *are* our future and it is imperative that we teach them well. However, I am not so sure the systems and structures of the public education system take into account this melodic mandate and we must begin to look past testing data and graduation rates.

For a very long time now, we have heard that a reform needs to happen in the public education system. And I do believe that many of us would agree that change is needed. We know that many problems exist in the public education system. As a matter of fact, we can see it with the most recent Presidential appointment for Secretary of Education and her vision for a new way to educate our young people; it has created an uproar because she represents a change in how we educate our young people.

The reason for this uproar is that what happens in the public school system involves and affects so many people. Yes, we know change is needed, however, we have not collectively found a real, promising new way to bring the necessary reform.

No matter what happens as it relates to reform in public education, one thing is certain; millions of lives are being touched every single day and our focus should be strategically targeted toward the people.

The Mountain of Education highlights the need for a foundational approach to looking at what we do within our families, our community, and our society, locally and globally. If our families are not functioning with the future in mind, they will not produce children ready for the future. If our communities don't incorporate an "it takes a village" mindset, then we will only push and protect our individual pursuits. When you consider how this affects our local and global societies, we are not truly valuing what education can do in its wider worldview perspective. Education broadens our perspectives. If our future is to be a successful one, as an individual, as a community, and as a society, then we must educate our young people with this in mind.

Personal Perspective

The issues plaguing public schools is hindering the work of educating our young people. Unfortunately, those issues encourage finger-pointing, frustration for parents and students, and burnout among the professionals in the school system.

As a parent with children in public schools and as an educator, my heart aches at seeing how students, parents, teachers, and administrators struggle to find hope in such conditions. Before we are able to get on with the business of educating students, we must identify these issues and deal with them.

Among the major issues, we see disrespect and dishonor for administrators and teachers, from parents and students. Teachers also feel that administrator support is lacking, making it very difficult to find joy in educating their students. And statistics show that teachers leave the profession for these reasons within the first five years of entering the profession.

Being an educator, I can tell you first-hand that teachers feel pressured and burdened by the weight of responsibility of educating our young people. Because the burden is a heavy one, the pressures coming from so many directions make it very difficult at times to continue showing up every day.

Students are also feeling the pressure of performing well on state exams and being tested so frequently, while they struggle to make sense of life outside of school because of absent parents, the need to overcome difficult things at home, and bullying and abuse from their peers and unfortunately the adults in their life while on school campuses around our nation.

The work that must go on in the schools is the state's issue, but those issues plaguing students, teachers, and administrators are Church issues. The Church has the responsibility of teaching love, modeling compassion and empathy, and equipping people with the tools they need to successfully interact with one another within a community. If the Church can focus its outreach efforts in a strategic way, we can begin to bridge the gap that has existed between schools within their local communities.

Church as a Community Connector

Schools belong to the community. What happens in our schools should always concern those who live in that community. Because people are at the heart of education and the Church has a mandate with people being its central focus, we need to look at the issues in educating our young people and issues affecting those who work as professionals in public schools, and how the Church can help bridge the gaps we see in the home-school-community partnership.

So, how can the Church be a part of what is happening in our schools?

The Church can be a very strong community connector, such that every believer working in the mountain of education should strive to be effective in its outreach efforts in bringing solutions to the problems that need to be addressed.

When we look at those issues affecting teachers and students, those are the matters that can, in fact, be addressed within families who accept responsibilities for their children's misbehavior. Objectively speaking, much of this issue can be attributed to the breakdown of the family.

The Church's role in the mountain of education also involves educating members in its community, concerning issues such as character, integrity, and submission to authority. If the Church would take an active role in bridging the gaps between those living in our communities, then those areas where life intersects, we could have purposeful and productive interactions with one another.

We absolutely cannot excuse the Church from the mountain of education because one of the offices of the fivefold ministry is that of a Teacher (Ephesians 4:11-12). The function of this office is to teach biblical principles. It is this lack of teaching in the home that does not allow students to go into their schools and classrooms and exhibit these moral standards.

Every Church within communities should have thriving marriage/family and youth ministries because these are the times that biblical principles can be taught to their members, who will then go into our schools, and who should exhibit those moral standards that come from learning biblical principles.

The separation of Church and state comes because of seeing the Church as a religious institution. However, the principles of Jesus help us to live life here on Earth. If we can be wise in our call to go into all the world, then the Church must change the way we approach ministry so that we can be strategic and very intentional in how we fulfill our "go ye into all the world" mandate.

Decrees and Declarations

1. I declare that, as a member of the Body of Christ, I am poised to make a difference in the lives of people who are part of the public school system.

2. I will partner with like-minded individuals to increase the Church's effectiveness in being a community-connector in every open door in the public school system, for the glory of God.
3. I will touch the lives of people in such a practical, yet powerful way, that lives will be forever changed. As partners with those laboring in the public school system, I will undergird their efforts at teaching our young people with intercessory prayer.
4. I will stand in the gap, petitioning Heaven for the necessary educational reform that will revolutionize the way we approach educating our young people.
5. I will give of my time, talents, and treasures to ensure that we meet critical needs and remove barriers to educating our young people.
6. I will exercise our dominion authority by using our voting power, so that we may position people in the political arena that will be governmental advocates for teachers and students.
7. I will not sit by and allow despair and devastation to overwhelm the frontline workers in public education. We are anointed change agents on the Earth and it's time for the Church to stand on the Mountain of Education and be a voice crying out for change!

---

[1] Moran, Rachel Nicole, "Education Reform: An Analysis of the purpose and function of public education." (2009). University of Tennessee Honors Thesis Projects. http://trace.tennessee.edu/utk_chanhonoproj/1300

[2] Flax, Bill, "The True Meaning of Separation of Church and State." (2011). Forbes.com. https://www.forbes.com/sites/billflax/2011/07/09/the-true-meaning-of-separation-of-church-and-state/#2bdf694d5d02

[3] National Center for Education Statistics, 2017. Back to School Fun Facts

DECODING THE HEALTH CRISES

By Shelby Frederick

Most physical ailments and diseases can be traced back to some unresolved and often hidden negative emotion and/or trauma from our childhood. Many people feel that they lack choices when it comes to their health decisions, but this is one area in which every person has direct control. According to Prevention Magazine, "It is estimated that 90 percent of all physical problems have psychological roots. That may sound like a gross exaggeration. In fact, it's probably a conservative estimate. A growing body of evidence indicates that virtually every ill that can befall the body—from acne to arthritis, headaches to heart disease, cold sores to cancer—is influenced, for better or worse, by our emotions" (Quoted from The Complete Guide To Your Emotions And Your Health). Our emotional health is just as important, if not more important than our physical health.

Nearly 50% of the U.S. population has one or more chronic health conditions, such as asthma, heart disease, obesity, cancer, or diabetes (2017 Employee Benefits Outlook, Wells Fargo). In the United States, it's estimated that two-thirds of adults are obese or overweight (Senior Researcher Dr. Bruce Lee, Associate Professor at the Johns Hopkins Bloomberg School of Public Health in Baltimore). Breast cancer is the most common form of cancer in the U.S., with an estimated 247,000 new cases reported in 2016, and an average paid claim amount of $147,100 (Sun Life Report, Sun Life Financial). 1 in 5 adults have a mental health condition (The State of Mental Health in America, MHA). More than one third of American adults are not getting enough sleep on a regular basis (CDC).

Adults reported that their physical and emotional symptoms due to stress increased 47% over the past year (APA Poll June 2008). This list is just a small representation of what's really going on in the lives of ordinary people like you and me on a daily basis.

With these staggering statistics, we can all agree that we are in a health crisis. How can we begin to reverse the trend of declining health in our society and put ourselves on the path to wholeness? In order to find the root, we must begin to work our way from the "outside in." We must find the open doors and close them so that we can begin to live 3 John 1:2 NLT which says, *"Dear friend, I hope all is well with you and that you are as healthy in body as you are strong in spirit."* With the health crisis reaching an all-time high, I would like to address what I feel is one of most important, but least talked about doors that lead to poor health. This is the door of our emotional wellness.

Emotions have a language. Emotions have energy. Emotions are meant to be expressed. Emotions can be positive or negative. Positive emotions make us feel happy and cheerful. When we experience positive emotions, we want to share them with the world. But what happens when we experience negative emotions? We hide and suppress them. If we release positive emotions, what happens to the negative ones that we hide? Remember, emotions have energy, so they must go somewhere. Author Karol Truman has a saying, "Feelings buried alive, never die!" So, when we don't learn how to deal with our negative emotions to ensure a healthy outcome, they become buried inside of us until the next traumatic event triggers their release.

So, what does this have to do with our health? EVERYTHING! "Feelings that we have buried and are completely unaware of are what create the challenges, the uneasiness, the dis-ease, the pain and the crisis's situations in our lives."

My Battle With Anemia

I can personally testify to the damaging effects of unresolved emotional stress that attributed to me being diagnosed with severe anemia in 2010.

"About 20 percent of women, and 50 percent of pregnant women, are in the club. Only three percent of men are iron deficient. The most common form of anemia—an insufficient number of red blood cells—is caused by iron deficiency. Its symptoms are similar to depression: fatigue, irritability, brain fog" (Everyday Health Nov 14, 2014).

For months, I had feelings of fatigue and brain fog. I was very moody and had recurrent bronchitis which would cause asthma flare ups. I knew that I had to do something when I began to experience dizziness. After an urgent care visit, I was sent to my primary care doctor for bloodwork, which revealed that my iron levels were dangerously low. I was immediately put on a high dosage of iron pills, but that caused other health issues. Eventually, my levels returned to normal and I began to feel a lot better. One point that I need to make is that, although I was properly diagnosed for the physical symptoms, no one ever addressed the emotional ones.

What I later discovered was, discouragement and apathy are two direct consequences of anemia. I was experiencing depression and didn't know it. It was affecting every area of my life. My work performance began to significantly decrease. There was trouble in my personal relationships and I had no energy to do the basic duties for my family. I was sinking and sinking fast. I thought I was just suffering from the physical symptoms but it was much deeper than that. It wasn't until I took a certification class and we talked about emotional clearing that I realized that my anemic condition was really rooted in unresolved emotional issues that surfaced during one of the most stressful times of life. Hearing this made me do further research so that I could begin to loose myself from the grip of the negative emotions that were trying to take me out physically. It was at that point that I made a decision to take control of not only my physical health, but my emotional health, too.

We can no longer remain silent about the traumas of our past. It is a literal deathtrap. But we have been given the power to reverse the curse by identifying the triggers that open the door to these diseases and speaking life according to Proverbs 18:21, *"Death and life are in the power of the tongue,*

And those who love it will eat its fruit."

God wants us to know that we are comprised of mind, body, soul, and spirit. Any deficiency in one area, affects the others. Homeostasis is defined as the tendency of the body to seek and maintain a condition of balance or equilibrium within its internal environment, even when faced with external changes. We can draw great wisdom from Ephesians 4:16 which states, *"from whom the whole body, joined and knit together by what every joint supplies, according to the effective working by which every part does its share, causes growth of the body for the edifying of itself in love."* We can no longer ignore our emotional health. We must look at each of these doors, crack the code by tracing the root, and educate people on how each of these units affects the other.

Keys to Cracking the Code

Managing diseases is not healing if it's not moving you towards wholeness. We must educate ourselves on what is good to eat. Proverbs 4:7 says, "Wisdom is the principal thing; therefore get wisdom: and with all thy getting, get understanding."

How can we build the lives of those we are endeavoring to impact when we ignore the physical state of our own being? If we want to live healthier lives, we must start identifying the triggers which will lead us to the negative emotions that perpetuate sickness and disease in the body.

The world is looking for answers to life situations and the burdens that they carry. In a world that appears to be void of peace, we have the solution! It is critical in this hour for us to tap into the spirit of wisdom, understanding, counsel, and might in the area of health and wellness. We must begin to take charge of our own health by challenging a system set up to feed us poison. We must return to our roots of Genesis 1:29 which says, "And God said, 'See, I have given you every herb that yields seed which is on the face of all the Earth, and every tree whose fruit yields seed; to you it shall be for food.'" Decoding the health crisis starts with the renewing of our minds and knowing that we have to power to walk in wholeness! "Whatever the mind can conceive and believe, it can achieve,"

Napoleon Hill. If you want to live John 3:1-2, see yourself whole. Speak wholeness. Live wholeness. Achieve wholeness today, in every area of life: mind, body, soul, and spirit!

Prayer Points and Declarations

1. I honor my body and treat it as a gift from God by attending yearly checkups, eating a well-balanced diet, and participating in a regular fitness program (1 Corinthians 6:19-20).
2. I declare wholeness to my body systems that they are properly functioning at an optimal level and supporting one another in good health. (Ephesians 4:16).
3. I will not claim any disease as my own by calling it "my" but will rather speak life and call my mind, body, soul, and spirit back into proper functioning (Proverbs 18:21).
4. I declare that my physical and spiritual health partner in the spirit to manifest good health in my body (3 John 1:2).
5. I declare restoration to every area of my physical health that has been compromised due to any unresolved emotional trauma (Jeremiah 30:17).
6. I declare a normal circulation of blood around my heart, arteries and veins that will give sufficient oxygen flow.

    I declare that because of Jesus Christ's finished work on the cross, every negative doctor's report must come subject to its authority (Psalms 73:26).

JUSTICE ON THE MOUNTAIN OF EDUCATION

By Joy Witter

AMERICA is that **ONE "NEW' NATION UNDER GOD**. As I climbed the Education Mountain, I addressed the issue of division and injustice. At the root of the issue is a lack of unity. There is a corporate anointing that God wants to release on the Earth in this hour. He is calling all seven cultural mountains of influence to unite for the glory of God. We, who were once separated from Christ and excluded from citizenship, have been brought near by the blood of Jesus. He has removed all barriers, including cultural, religious, racial, and social ones. There is no need for injustice, division, racism, inequality, or segregation to permeate our education system. According to Ephesians 2:14, hostility and hatred have been confronted and defeated by Jesus' sacrifice on the cross.

This anthology is summoning educators of the nations to arise. As kings and priests, walking in our true identity, we are called to dominate our specific mountain; to speak with power and authority so that things change when we speak. God is doing a new thing to bring a "new nation" together out of the many people groups, just as the Lord did for the Jews and Gentiles, in Ephesians 2:11. The cross is a game-changer. There is no more separation between God's people. There is power in agreement and coming together as one.

The effects of injustice, segregation, and race issues are evident in our education system and consequently our nation, for many centuries. We have been called as a Kingdom of Kings and Priests and light-bearers, to dispel darkness and to destroy the works of the devil. This is evident as I travel across regions and territories. I recall a story about unity that marked my life in 2009 when I was in Missouri. I had a personal revelation about Ephesians 2:11-23.

One day, I called the realtor for a house I saw advertised. I needed a home of my own. I didn't have money but by faith, I believed this need would be met. So, I went to look at homes. Little did I know that it was an opportunity to *minister* to the realtor. It was an hour both ways to see the house. I started to share the revelation of how the cross removed the wall of hostility and there is now equality, unity, and diversity instead. Now, every culture, nation, and race can cross the line to have access to God the Father. The presence and power of God showed up as I began to speak and the man was being swept into sobbing. This was a white man of high caliber, on the church board, who taught many people and went to a famous church in the area. I didn't earn the right to speak to him. I was not in his class in no way. But God has put treasures in earthen vessels. The man told me not to take myself lightly because God had used me mightily that day to teach him an object lesson.

The manifestation of the new nation requires an upgrade in Kingdom identity. Our vision and perspective of ourselves and assignment need to be carried out. Based on the paradigm that "if you want to change a nation, begin with the education system," God has called us to "dwell together in unity." This is what I hear the Holy Spirit saying to the remnant in this hour. Kingdom citizens have to take dominion and authority to speak to the effects of the moral decadence which our education system has promoted whether consciously or unconsciously.

As I sought the face of God, this critical issue of injustice becomes the most dominant in my spirit, and I felt the drive to speak on the mountain top. As one that is called to advance the pursuit of knowledge, unity at all levels of education is needed. As revealed to me, there is a desperate cry for unity in education and our nation, and even all over the globe. If the *"kingdom of the world is to become the Kingdom of our Lord and of his Christ"* (Revelation 11:15), we must demonstrate that we are one in Christ. There is no division; the blood of Jesus paid it in full for all humans to have access to God the Father.

The solution to the issue is **unity**. This is the message I have lived for 12 years and I'm still proclaiming. Unity is directly related to identity, diversity, equality, and equity. This will influence society for the Kingdom of God as a resolution and reversal of past legislation of Church and state separate.

In order to promote unity, I needed to have an identity and fulfill my assignment to be a light to the dark world. This was evident as I began to embrace Isaiah 49:6 and "light to the Nations" jumped out at me. One day, I went to volunteer at a school in Missouri. An eight-year-old boy had a melt-down. He began to say: "I won't be anything when I grow up, I only want to be the light bulb." I asked him to come with me to another room and I used the same things he was talking about to tell him a story about Jesus. I told him Jesus was homeless, knocking at the door of his heart, and if he would let Him in, Jesus could make him a light. He said a prayer and received Jesus into his heart. I led him to declare out loud: "Jesus loves me, Jesus is the light of the world. I have power like Jesus." The light bulb in the room went out in that instant. The boy became convinced that he has a greater purpose. God began to customize my life and walk and used me as a light to many people.

Promoting unity in education can bring the Kingdom of God here in America and cause a domino effect across the four corners of the Earth. America will be that One "New" Nation under God. She will be aligned with the Pledge of Allegiance and be in congruency with finally living it out. There is no need for division. It is time to be that one new nation under God, indivisible because in truth and in fact we are. Why shouldn't it be the remnant, who are sanctified and Holy Ghost-filled? I prophesy that we have the victory in the education system of our nation. Speaking these declarations of unity will bring our society into divine alignment.

Why Unity?

Injustice or racism can be subtle, but the impact leaves scars on the soul of a person. The key to resolving the issue is not getting into political or religious arguments about Church and state being separate. The solution lies in the ability of a nation to unite, forgive, overcome indifferences, and embrace diversity. The purpose is to unite in purpose "one nation under God" just as the Pledge of Allegiance states. When we unite our vision and purpose beyond ideologies, philosophies, and other earthly things, the will of God is accomplished. Anointed as a light, we all become a voice that speaks as the oracles of God, to declare and use kingdom strategies to impact the education mountain and bring unity, identity, diversity, and equity. The long-term effect will be a restoration of moral conscience, core values, and children living with purpose and fulfilling destinies.

Jesus has already destroyed the hostile dividing wall between nations. We have no choice but to unite because we are one. No matter how we think about what happens between us, we are united. The cross is the game-changer. It reconciled us back to God. We have the same Maker and He sees us through the eyes of His grace.

Prayers and Prophetic Decrees

1. Heavenly Father, we repent for America, and the sin of division and injustice.
2. Lord, bring unity to our education system in Jesus' Name.
3. Lord, preserve our generations, bring equity and diversity in Jesus' name.
4. We cry out for the souls of our children. Lord, help America to be one new nation under God.
5. We beseech you, Lord, change our hearts, teach us to love every race, color, class, and embrace diversity.
6. We decree and declare that division and hostility is washed away by the blood of Jesus.
7. We declare that the seeing eyes of God watch over our schools and strengthen our leaders (1Chronicles 16:9)
8. We declare that the Lord watches over his Word to perform it (Jeremiah 1:12) change is here
9. Lord, bring deliverance to the education system as you did for Mount Zion in (Joel 2:32).

10. I decree and declare; our children are preserved by the anointing of oneness.
11. Holy Spirit, unleash a fresh anointing upon the education mountain that will impart a fresh revelation about your power to reconcile nations.

---

[1] Maldonado, Guillermo. The Kingdom of Power: How to Demonstrate it Here & Now. Whittaker House. 2013.

[2] www.partnerwithschools.org/separation-of-church-and-state.html

[3] http://teachersinstitute.yale.edu/curriculum/units/2004/1/04.01.03.x.html

[4] http://compelledtoact.com/Tragic_listing/Main_listing_victims.htm

[5] www.christianpost.com/author/eric-metaxas/ ONE NATION UNDER GOD

[6] By Eric Metaxas Sep 17, 2012 9:28 AM. Date accessed 10.05.2017

CHAPTER 4

THE MOUNTAIN OF ARTS & ENTERTAINMENT

This mountain is one of the most powerful and influential forces that affect and shape our culture today, especially our youth. Not only is the Education Mountain discipling the next generation, but this mountain may even be yielding more influence over young people. We are talking about movies, TV, music, poetry, fashion, sports, and other forms of entertainment. This mountain is also referred to as the Celebration Mountain. Hollywood is one of the most powerful of them all, having global influence on an entire generation. Remember, it is only a small group of 3-8% that determines what happens on the tops of these mountains. It is said that only about 200 people decide what kinds of films Hollywood will produce. Look at how Hip Hop has become a sub-cultural phenomenon, exported from the U.S. to other parts of the world now for close to two decades. You will find Hip Hop in Cairo, Johannesburg, Moscow, Delhi, and Kathmandu—in every nation and major city.

Our problem in the Church has been that we wanted all the talented people on this mountain who came to Christ, to camp out in the Church. We didn't equip and disciple them to become Kingdom influencers of culture with their gifts. But that is now changing. A major paradigm shift is taking place in the Church. More and more biblically-based and inspired movies are being produced. Hollywood has been finding out that there is a huge market for it, and these movies are profitable. Christian singers, rappers, and musicians are discovering that many of them are called beyond serving in the four walls of the Church on Sunday morning to being a light of influence on this cultural mountain through their gifts and talents. This mountain has shifted the values of our culture further and further away from a biblical worldview. Now it's time for that to be reversed.

THE INTENT AND PURPOSE OF THE ARTS

By Niles Bess

Music, sound, artistic expression, and movement were always intended to glorify God. Music and movement are of the most powerful communication tools God has provided.

In the beginning, God created the most beautiful creature that was full of wisdom. The creature was Lucifer. He was also full of sounds and music. Before his fall, Lucifer's original purpose as a Cherub was to cover and guard the very throne of God.

Ezekiel 28:12-16

"'You were the seal of perfection, full of wisdom and perfect in beauty. [13]You were in Eden, the garden of God; every precious stone adorned you: carnelian, chrysolite and emerald, topaz, onyx and jasper, lapis lazuli, turquoise and beryl. Your settings and mountings were made of gold; on the day you were created they were prepared. [14]You were anointed as a guardian cherub, for so I ordained you. You were on the holy mount of God; you walked among the fiery stones. [15]You were blameless in your ways from the day you were created till wickedness was found in you. [16]Through your widespread trade you were filled with violence, and you sinned. So I drove you in disgrace from the mount of God, and I expelled you, guardian cherub, from among the fiery stones."

As we see in the above scripture, Lucifer had the awesome responsibility of providing worship for the throne room of Heaven. Once he was expelled and thrown out, that responsibility shifted to man. Because of that shift, we are responsible for creating and releasing glorious sounds, dance, and expressions that honor and glorify God.

This is why it's imperative that we understand the purpose of musicians, singers, artists, and dancers in this season. In II Kings, Elisha the prophet called upon a minstrel to play so that he could hear the Word of the Lord concerning Jehoshaphat the king of Judah. This was significant. Elisha needed an open Heaven in order to hear what God was saying, which could only happen with a minstrel.

By definition, musicians are those who compose, conduct, or perform music. Minstrels are those that play stringed instruments; a musician/player with the grace and anointing to move the hand of God when they play. *(Bess, N. A. (2011)*

From Heaven to Earth

The King of Glory and God of all creation has given us the ability to be creative. Again, our creativity is intended to glorify God. When we look at the mountain of arts and entertainment, we see the ungodly influences that flood our eye and ear gates. One of the names of Satan is "The prince of the power of the air". *("The Holy Bible." YouVersion, 2002-2017; Ephesians 2:2 (KJV))*

The Scripture goes on to say that this is *"the spirit that now worketh in the children of disobedience."* One of the key reasons why it's important to monitor what you listen to and what you watch is the fact that the music is the one thing that does not need your permission to enter you. Even if you are not paying attention and listening actively, the frequency and sound waves will penetrate your soul and subconsciously, you will begin to hum, tap your feet, etc.

As those that are called to this mountain mature in their abilities, they will need to learn how to tap into the heavenly realm to access the art that needs to be released on the Earth. Understanding the access point of the River of Heaven that makes glad the city of God, is key! *("The Holy Bible." YouVersion, 2002-2017; Psalms 46:4 (KJV))*

In order to influence this mountain, God has raised more Chenaniah's on the Earth. Chenaniah is also known as "master of the song" which would be considered the equivalent of today's modern producer. He not only was the music director and producer, but he also had rule over the city of Israel with his sons. The influence that God gives you will go beyond your artistic expression.

1 Chronicles 26:29 (KJV) - *"Of the Izharites, **Chenaniah** and his sons were for the outward business over Israel, for officers and judges."*

Reclaiming Arts and Entertainment for the Kingdom

Reclaiming the arts and entertainment for the Kingdom has to be a top priority for those called to this area. It will take strategy and commitment to excellence to make this happen. When comparing the Church productions to the mainstream offerings, more often than not, the Church and/or believers are falling short in the quality and excellence department. If we are to be taken seriously, we must bring quality products and cutting-edge strategies to the table.

As we continue to focus more on the Kingdom offering versus "Church" or "religious" offering, we will begin to secure more ground in this area of influence.

Prayer Points

1. I will Worship and create new expressions to God to open doors and purpose in my life. (Psalm 34:9 MSG)
2. I decree the Kingdom of God reigns over the Mountain of Arts & Entertainment. (Psalm 48:1 KJV)
3. The River of Heaven shall influence the Kingdoms of the world. (Psalm 46:4 KJV)
4. Those that are called to influence the Mountain of Arts & Entertainment shall be rooted and grounded in His presence and shall bring forth fruit. (Psalm 1:3 KJV)
5. Let revelation and the mysteries of God be released through His prophets and minstrels. (2 Kings 3:15 KJV)
6. Let humility be the portion of those in leadership and those that have

influence within the mountains. (1 Corinthians 1:29 KJV)
7. Strength and gladness shall be with those called to influence the mountain of Art and Entertainment. (1 Chronicles 16:27 KJV)
8. The King of Glory shall fight the battle of those carrying His banner. (Psalm 24:8 KJV)
9. Let every area of the arts glorify God. (Psalm 150:4 KJV)
10. Let the Presence of the Lord dwell upon the mountain of Arts and Entertainment. (Psalm 68:16 KJV)
11. Let the Tabernacle of David be rebuilt and the breach closed. (Amos 9:11 KJV)
12. Let the Earth shine with the glory of God. (Ezekiel 43:2 KJV)

---

[1] Bess, N. A. (2011). *Minstrels and Psalmists: The Key to Davidic Praise and Worship* (pp. 10-11). Chicago, IL: Author House Publishing.

[2] "The Holy Bible." YouVersion, 2002-2017, https://www.bible.com Accessed 10 Dec. 2017.

[3] *Story of Lucifer*, All About God, 2002-2017, https://www.allaboutgod.com/story-of-lucifer.htm Accessed 8 Dec. 2017

SUBLIMINAL MESSAGES ON THE MOUNTAIN OF ENTERTAINMENT

By Michelle Jackson

Entertainment is used to subliminally influence all cultures through music, movies, spoken word, dance, drama, social media, television, and storytelling, by holding the attention and interest of an audience. The body of Christ has lost much influence on the Mountain of Arts & Entertainment. The enemy often works through human agents on this mountain to produce evil and perverted values that influence the cultures, resulting in a rapid decline in morals and rapid increase of demonic activity. Satan uses entertainment to limit a person's imagination, meaning, and purpose in life. What a person repeatedly hears and sees, they become. Proverbs 4:23 (NIV) says, *"Above all else, guard your heart, for everything you do flows from it."* Luke 11:34 says, *"Your eye is a lamp that provides light for your body."* Entertainment that is ungodly will transform your mind and spirit man with darkness. Whoever controls your mind, is your *god*.

Entertainment should reflect the glory and majesty of God. 2 Chronicles 5:11-14 speaks of the fact that, when God hears true entertainment in the Earth realm, He releases His glory. Verse 13 says, *"It came even to pass, as the trumpeters and singers were as one, to make one sound to be heard in praising and thanking the Lord; and when they lifted up their voice with trumpets and cymbals and instruments of music, and praised the Lord, saying, For he is good; for his mercy endureth for ever: that them the house was filled with a cloud, even the house of the Lord."* God intended for the Church to be the governing body with great influence in every sphere that makes up society. The

Church is to expand Heaven on Earth in ministerial efforts that include entertainment.

Music, television, and social media are the most influential forces on the Mountain of Entertainment. The use of the three has distorted the standards and ethical values in many individuals between the ages of ten to the early twenty's. Adolescents and teenagers are the groups affected the most by the impurity in entertainment. Many young African-American boys believe gangster rap music and videos are a reality. The jailhouses are full of young men that admired violence, drugs, and the degrading of women. The strong appeal of drugs, alcohol, and sex goes against everything God stands for. It can also produces gender confusion. The enemy's plan is if he shows enough *gender change* on this Mountain, people will begin to believe this is normal. Many within this age group have made idols out of the men/women in the music, TV, and film industry.

This is leading a generation into the pits of hell! This is rebellion against God and He will destroy the idols in the land. Zechariah 13:2 says, *"And it shall come to pass in that day, saith the Lord of hosts, that I will cut off the names of the idols out of the land, and they shall no more be remembered."* We need to have strong, powerful, God-fearing men and women to infiltrate the entertainment industry; those that will not sell out for fame, but use their God-given talents in this arena while exemplifying godly character. When God's people get into position, they can change the fabric of the entertainment culture. What we behold is what we become. The expression of God needs to be put into the Entertainment Mountain for a maximum impact that will deliver, set free, and release millions of souls from darkness into the marvelous light. When entertainment is infused with the power of God, the glory of God will be released.

The body of Christ needs to be prophetic in music, song, acting, dancing, and poetry. The prophetic insight and leading from the Holy Spirit will release an anointing that can be used as a weapon of warfare. The Holy Spirit will remind you and lead you to set personal boundaries so that you will not be in a place where God does not want you. When a person diligently seeks God, He will promote and place them on top of the Mountain to reign and establish the culture of the Kingdom.

Prayer

Father God, we come to you in the name of your son, Jesus. Teach us how to move under the power and covering of the Holy Spirit. Release godly wisdom and discernment that will allow us to take back the Mountain of Entertainment. Allow the ones that are deeply rooted in you, who will not sell out for fame, to control Hollywood. Empower the body of Christ that they will not feel defeated, weak, or confused. Remind them that they are your end-time warriors. I cancel and rebuke the spirits of perversion, paramecia, lust, vanity, fame, covetousness, and idolatry, and command you, foul spirits to go back to the pits of hell in Jesus' name.

Father, birth your artistic ability into the Earth realm that will bring pleasure and break all demonic strongholds. I decree that the Mountain of Entertainment will bring a refreshing and renewing of minds/emotions. Let there be a reflection of the glory and beauty of God through what we see and hear. I decree that the body of Christ is the salt and light of the world, the pillar of society. Open the eyes of the saints to the dominion and authority that has been given to us; we will not lose sight of our purpose on Earth. Amen.

In the name of Jesus, I break off any limitations and restrictions that were placed on my soul through my involvement, knowingly or unknowingly, in movies, literature, music, or spoken word. Father, remove all the darkness that we have seen with our eyes and heard with our ears and purge and purify us with the blood of Jesus (Proverb 4:23 & Luke 11:34).

Decrees & Declarations

1. I decree that God will cut down all the idols of the land that are causing people to turn their heart away from God (2 Chronicles 34:7). I decree this in Jesus' name.
1. Sprinkle clean water upon us and cleanse us from all filthiness, and cleanse us from all idols (Ezekiel 36:25).

2. I decree that every evil Mountain that has been established in the entertainment industry hear and obey the voice of God (Micah 6:2).
3. Father, we need the power and might from your hand to be released against every stronghold that has an influence over the Mountain of Entertainment (1 Chronicles 29:12).
4. I release the power and authority of the LORD against all demons that I have encountered unknowingly through music, and all forms of entertainment (Matthew 10:1).
5. I rebuke and cast out any spirit that would attempt to oppress me through the media in Jesus' name.
6. Father, release the sword out of your mouth against the enemy that promotes violence, destruction of my soul, sexual perversion, racism, and hatred through entertainment (Revelation 19:15).
7. I command all spirits of witchcraft that work with lust through the media to release your grip now. I decree this in Jesus' name.
8. I decree and break every demonic soul tie of my life that will keep me bound to all ungodly covenants established by listening to and hearing subliminal messages in the media.

A PROPHETIC VOICE ON THE MOUNTAIN OF ARTS & ENTERTAINMENT

By Dr. James Pinto

Some people have a prophetic voice and are hiding, while others are prophetic and have been hidden by God. Regardless of what group you are in, it is time to arise and shine and let your voice be heard. God has deposited a special gift inside of you and He expects to see you live life as an instrument of love and peace. He gave us His Son Jesus as an example for us to imitate. The gift is not just for us, but for the benefit of others. We have the responsibility to activate, revive, and awaken our talents, so we will be a voice of influence wherever we are, but specifically in our field of expertise.

When we hear the expression, *speak to the mountains*, we may immediately think there is a problem, an obstacle, or a very stressful situation that needs to be removed from our lives or simply disappear. Even though it might be a valid point, as an artist, my focus will not be how to make the evil people in the Arts and Entertainment Mountain cease to exist, but rather how to reach and influence them, and restore the voice that has been stolen from us.

John the Baptist had a specific assignment as a forerunner and pioneer. It was to be the voice that would announce and prepare the coming of Jesus. Similarly, we also have a role as artists in our sphere of influence, and it is to prepare the way for God's glory to be manifested in tangible ways in a field where intellect and pride have tried to suffocate God's existence and presence.

We tend to view and analyze people and their actions based on our religious background, upbringing, ethnicity, personal experiences, and family values. Sociologist James Q. Wilson reveals the following fact, "On city streets where broken windows have gone unrepaired, the crime rate immediately soars. Why? The broken windows make an announcement to the public: Here standards have broken down. Here no authority applies. Come and do what you like without consequences."

The enemy has assaulted the arts and entertainment industry and broken the moral values of our society. The Bible describes in John 10:10, *"The thief comes only to steal and kill and destroy; I have come that they may have life, and have it to the full."* There is such confusion about what is right and wrong in today's society. We as Christian artists need to take a stand and bring Heaven on Earth and restore the abundant life that God intended originally for humanity. That life includes clarity of mind to make right choices, raising the standards of integrity, and being a light in the dark with our actions not only words. The enemy has also removed or counterfeited God's authority in the industry. It seems that whatever messages come from major films, fashion, and music, led by celebrity icons, have the final say and should not be challenged.

God is calling his artists to take authority over the spirits of deception and pride, and bring truth in love. In doing so, His authority will be manifested as mentioned in Philippians 2:9-11, *"Therefore God exalted him to the highest place and gave him the name that is above every name, that at the name of Jesus every need should bow, in heaven, and on earth, and under the earth, and every tongue acknowledge that Jesus Christ ids Lord, to the glory of the Father."* The enemy has blinded the eyes of many producers, actors, models, singers, and musicians, making them believe that there are no consequences for their actions and they believe that "no restraint at all" means freedom. If we are not careful, we as well might become easy prey and compromise our beliefs, identity, and foundations. We as Christian artists have the responsibility to lead by carrying a mantle of holiness and conviction. We are accountable to God first then men. *"We must obey God rather than men"* (Acts 5:29). God is the Creator of arts and He will not use them to destroy, but to uplift, encourage, and bring hope.

Karen Covell, the founder of Hollywood Prayer Network, refers to Hollywood as the most influential mission field in the world. I tend to agree after seeing how the music, film, and fashion industries, to name a few, have penetrated our society in such a powerful way. As I pray, meditate, and tune my ears to what God is saying about the Arts and Entertainment, it is very clear to me that He is to rallying his troops, gathering his eagles, and bringing His prophets into a new place we have not been before. God wants to release strategies, designs, and messages, and also give access to doors that have been shut for many years.

I am convinced that the time is now and we have to be ready to go when God says, "Go." We will know that we are ready when we start operating under the same Spirit of unity, compassion, love, and godly character. Division, criticism, judgment, rivalry, jealousy, competition, and self-righteousness are not going to be helpful in this season. We already have those traits and spirits in the Arts and Entertainment and it is not a good thing to replicate them, but rather bring the opposite spirit.

When we as artists offer an alternative filled with excellence, high standards, skills second to none, coupled with humility and authority, we will gain ground and be of great influence among those who are currently in key places. It is not enough to be Spirit-filled and it is not enough to be academic-ready, though we need both. It is no longer this or that, but this and that. God will use every single type of training and educational background available, but with a glory mantle that will dismantle the counterfeit of the enemy.

For so long, we have remained passive and watched what we are passionate about and what we were born to do, remain out of reach and impossible to achieve. God is awakening us, stirring those dreams that He implanted in our hearts, and fulfilling His promises as He said. He is a promise-keeper, a faithful finisher, and a loving father. Get ready to arise and shine—no more passivity, no more complacency, no more indifference, and no more frustration-driven life. The shift is here and we have to move and advance with it.

I am going to make some declarations and decrees over the Mountain of

Arts and Entertainment trusting that God will honor and cover them with His presence until the day they become a reality.

Decrees & Declarations

1. I decree and declare that all the resources available in the music industry will be available for God's prophetic artists.
2. I decree and declare that the prophetic will invade Nashville and Hollywood in ways that will confuse the enemy.
3. I decree and declare that we will find the other 7,000 prophets that have been hiding and partner with them to complete the assignment.
4. I decree and declare that we will reach the highest positions of honor in the industry and bring God's influence and glory into the Arts and Entertainment industry.
5. I decree and declare that Jezebel will be dethroned and replaced by true prophets at the top of the Mountain.
6. I decree and declare that the eyes and ears of those Christian leaders with influence in Hollywood and Nashville will open the doors to the prophetic.
7. I decree and declare that the voice of music will shift and affect the rest of the Mountains.
8. I decree and declare that the voice of fashion will manifest, bringing new stylists, creative fashionistas, and models who will prophesy with their creativity.
9. I decree and declare that films, producers, and actors will create more awareness in the prophetic.
10. I decree and declare that the level of creativity in the people of God will increase and even hold hands with other movements in Europe, Asia, Africa, Australia, and the rest of the world.
11. I decree and declare that we will move with wisdom, humility, and authority in the Arts and Entertainment industry.
12. I decree and declare that the blood of Jesus will break any curses that have been cast upon God's artists and their creativity.
13. I decree and declare that we will occupy our rightful place in the Mountain, and receive the highest honor and awards prepared for us

before the foundation of the world.
14. I decree and declare that we will be the recipients of inheritances and transfer of wealth for Kingdom purposes.
15. I decree and declare that new businesses in film, fashion, and music will surface.
16. I decree and declare that we will no longer be rejected by the industry.
17. I decree and declare that God's holy name will be exalted above any other name as it is in Heaven. In the mighty name of Jesus, Amen!

CHAPTER 5

THE MOUNTAIN OF RELIGION

Some have called this: 1) the Christian Church mountain, while others have included in this mountain 2) all "religions" and see it more as the mountain dealing with all kinds of spiritual influences, including Christianity as a whole (Catholic, Orthodox, and Protestant), plus Buddhism, Islam, Judaism, Hinduism, Confucianism, New Age, Wicca, Occult, Secular Humanism, etc. My preference is the second option. According to Isaiah 2:1-5 and Micah 4:1-5, Zion, the Kingdom of God, or the Mountain of the Lord's Temple will be established as chief, or highest, or ruler of the other mountains, and all nations will flow to it. All true followers of Christ—the true *ekklesia* (Church)—are the true maturing "sons of God" who are functioning as "kings and priests" and developing the attitude and characteristics of the "overcomers" of Revelation chapters 2 and 3, and building a spiritual house of prayer for all nations, along with their intimacy as friends of Jesus (the King's inner circle of friends). They are the ones ruling and reigning with Christ on the tops of the mountains.

The Mountain of Religion is the mountain which for thousands of years has influenced cultures and nations through any number of "spiritual" influences, whether for good or bad. Even though much damage has been done in the name of *Christianity* in many nations, that was not in line with Scripture and Christ's ideals. A true ekklesia of Jesus' followers that model Christ both in His earthly servant leadership Lamb nature, along with His heavenly Kingly Lion nature, will be required to witness against principalities and powers and spiritual wickedness in high places on the

Mountain of Religion. A powerful conversation needs to be had in terms of what that looks like on the mountains of influence.

The Church, by and large, is losing the battle of influencing cultures and nations, even though in America and other countries, we have so many megachurches. And yet, when you measure the true transformation in those cities with the most megachurches, the statistics reveal minimal transformation. We are doing a relatively good job at populating Heaven, but rather poorly at transforming the Earth. The Bible speaks of healing nations and discipling nations, but it seems we are not really doing a great job at that. Where is the disconnect? It's somewhere in the understanding of our role as the ekklesia on the Earth that has been called to rule mountains with Christ.

In many nations where the Church is growing quickly, it has a lot of influence on the Mountain of Religion, as it begins to outshine all other competing belief systems. But now for transformation to take place, it must truly understand the mandate "on Earth as it is in Heaven" and see how an ekklesia of sons and daughters of God can be planted on each of the other mountains of culture to transform society.

Jesus, in Matthew 16, chose a Greek governmental term, "ekklesia," to introduce this new concept of "Church"—a governing body of sons and daughters of God. The Mountain of Religion is potentially the greatest mountain of cultural change. But the true Church on this mountain must remain true to Scripture in order to be the city of light set upon a hill shining in the darkness.

THE EAGLE ANOINTING: MANTLED TO DESTROY OPPRESSION IN CULTS

By LaDonna Jackson

Many who have been marked by God, are what I call *change agents*. They have the capacity to change atmospheres and environments around them. Another name for these carriers of glory is *eagles*. These eagles excel in detecting and dismantling cults and false religions on the Mountain of Religion. Later on, you will see that wherever there is counterfeit religion, there will also be sexual immorality. My charge is to expound on various forms of sexual oppression (sexual bondage via sex-trafficking, pedophilia, ritualistic sex, and abuse) in cults that in reality disguise themselves as churches, then I will offer eagles' strategies to defeat it.

There has been a sinister trend introduced in some churches under the guise of spiritual sonship, and tribal likeliness, called sexual oppression. When a spiritual leader uses his/her authority to impose their sexuality onto someone that they lead, it is the practice of occultism. This type of organization is not governed by the Church of Jesus Christ, but rather the kingdom of darkness, or a cult. While we often see this practiced in organizations such as small sects of Mormonism, and some parishes within Catholicism, I would like to focus on the hidden mysticism within some Christian circles. According to Mark 4:22 RSV, "For there is nothing hid, except to be made manifest; nor is anything secret, except to come to light." Therefore, I believe it is most appropriate to share highlights of my personal testimony of how I survived a cult.

While pursuing my Master's at a university away from home, I began following a widely-known ministry. The minister I began to follow was likened to Charles Manson; charismatic, smart, incommensurable against the norm, and authoritative. He reached out to me over social media and I later learned that he had been surveying me from afar, only to prey on me. He soon won my trust and initiated me into a core group with like-minds, callings, and broken pasts. Although I was told that I was going to be hired as the only female in the "ministry's" inner circle, I wasn't the only one in his life. He was married, and lived a double life. He literally, in his own words, "clocked in at eight, and clocked out at five." I was not allowed around his wife, nor was I encouraged to speak to my parents about him.

Soon thereafter, my core beliefs in the truth of Jesus Christ were challenged and washed away in a matter of four months. Because I had a slave mentality and thought I could not survive without a master, I submitted at an accelerated pace. The minister and I soon became intimate. I learned there was another young woman in the "ministry"—that was concealed from the rest of us—and had been intimate with him for at least 20 years. Once I found out about this particular young woman, a trail of secrets began to unfold. His animal-hunting hobby was actually a cover-up for an occult practice called blood sacrifice. He used it to astral project to certain individuals' homes at night. He had a lair in his home full of my pictures, where he performed rituals, as well as a gun collection with which he threatened to kill me if I ever told anyone about his lifestyle. After several attempts to escape on my own with no success, I had to tell someone so that they could help me. Through this experience, I learned how to discern what a cult entailed.

CULT INDICATORS:

1. Teaching indicates that lewd, sexual behavior is acceptable as some deep spiritual truth.
2. The authority convinces you that the sexual acts you consent to are your fault.
3. You discover that many, if not all members of the group, have severely dysfunctional/broken pasts.

4. The speech amongst the group is similar, and many times vulgar.
5. The group truly believes that they carry a special and elevated truth.
6. The authority encourages you to separate yourself from your loved ones by promoting self-sufficiency and arrogance.
7. The organization is built on and secured by secrets.
8. You become desensitized to false teaching.
9. The authority will never permit you to succeed to a greater spiritual level than him/her, as they are intimidated by your calling.
10. The higher you are promoted in the organization, the more rewards you obtain, and the more corrupt it appears to be.
11. They reinforce unbiblical principles that may have spiritual, psychological, emotional, physical, and cultural consequences; ex. not taking birth control.
12. You are affirmed to be initiated into the group, only to have your weaknesses exposed at a later time, or maybe even used against you if you don't comply with the rules of the organization; the strategy is to build you up, then tear you down.
13. It is very difficult to leave the organization, because it can be life-threatening.

If you survey every cult indicator listed above, you can observe that the parallels between the pimp and the prostitute (which is modern slavery), and my testimony are quite similar. Whether on the streets or in what seems to be Church, bondage is bondage. While visiting a local anti-sex trafficking educational agency, I learned that in order to break the minds of prostitutes, pimps would take them into *breaking rooms*, with minimal food and water for up to seven days. We can give the enemy our minds before we give him our bodies. Over time, this would open the door for Stockholm syndrome.[1] There are studies that demonstrate that the faith community is even more vulnerable to abuse than secular environments. The Abel and Harlow study revealed that 93% of sex offenders describe themselves as "religious," and that this category of offenders may be the most dangerous. Other studies have found that sexual abusers within faith communities have younger victims.

Throughout biblical history and modern accounts, idolatry has always set the precedence for sexual perversion. The temple prostitutes (female or male slaves) would have sex with the worshippers to honor their select god. They were practicing what is known in the occult as *sex magic*. When a man ejaculates, he releases verbal incantations into the spirit realm of what he desires to manifest on Earth, albeit love, power, or wealth. What they were actually conjuring up was a demonic spirit that could grant them the aforementioned desires of their heart. Whenever there is a display of idolatry, as there commonly is in cults, there will always be heightened forms of sexual immorality amongst spiritual authority, and someone labeled as a son or daughter. This is a form of control. When I was submitted to my leader, I was under such a form of control that pulled me back into the organization, after he released incantations while holding my hand, the moment I told him that I wanted to leave. This is the power of sex and mind control. He was only allotted this amount of control, as I had given it to him in a backslidden condition.

As a Kingdom, we must progress beyond research in witchcraft if we desire to know the mind of God concerning cults. In order to receive data from Heaven, we must lean on intercession. The only type of vessel that can fly high enough, battle, and win against this force of hell, is an eagle. I like to compare an eagle with a general in an army. In order to win a battle against the enemy, the general must obtain *intel* from the opposing side. Then, he must decide on weaponry, strategies, front men, and finally, the end game.

Prayer Points for Those Who Have Once Fallen Prey

1. I bind the separation of personalities and damaged emotions that come as a result of sexual abuse from a spiritual father/mother.
2. I bind the guilt and shame that comes as a result of participating in the sexual act with their spiritual father/mother.
3. I bind and expel the orphan spirit that is reinforced during and after trauma, and I release love and acceptance that comes from God. Erase fear, and begin to heal impetuously. (2 Timothy 1:7)
4. I bind the spirit of the temple prostitute, also known as pride and idolatry of the orphan, that places the needs of their leader above the needs of ABBA Father. (Matthew 6:21-24)

5. May those who have severely dearth pasts become cycle breakers, and miracle makers in their family bloodlines! The curse of the "dysfunctional/broken" soul will cease with them.
6. May the damage of the *breaking room* be recalled and overturned in the name of Jesus!
7. Give the souls that are bound the courage to get out! (Romans 6:18)
8. I silence the curses of the enemy who torments them with lies that proclaim "you will be punished if you speak out against us" and loose the tongues of the gifted ones. May they have the courage to tell their story.
9. I bind the spirit of double-mindedness that threatens the destiny of the gifted ones. May they never fall prey as a result of false affirmation, followed by demonic verbal abuse from their spiritual authority. (James 1:6-8)
10. I pray that the spirit of rebellion will not take root, and there will be a healthy outlook on spiritual authority going forward.

Prophetic Declarations for the Eagle

1. FRONTMEN: We, as pioneers and forerunners, lead out against extreme opposition. (Matthew 14:29)
2. WEAPONRY: (Fear of God)

    We have a holy reverence for God.

3. WEAPONRY: (Holiness)

    We turn away from hidden and blatant sin in our lives. (John 21:17-18 NASB)

4. STRATEGY: (Intent for miracles)

    We become intentional about making room for His miraculous power to move in our churches.

5. STRATEGY & WEAPONRY: (Giant)

    We change our perspectives to fit a giant's purview. As our responsibilities expand, we view things from a different perspective. We will do whatever it takes: pray with keener vision, fast more and with apt listening abilities, and navigate better in the spiritual realm.

6. STRATEGY & INTEL: (Community)

   We connect with other eagles to combine intelligence and produce a means for the broken to get healed. (Luke 15:17-20)

7. STRATEGY & INTEL: (A watchmen's eye)

   Like watchmen, we sit on the wall, and monitor who poses a threat as they come in and out of the regional and household gates. (2 Samuel 18:24-29)

8. END GAME: (The attack)

   We stay above ground, and only come down to fight; we don't battle against flesh and blood. (Ephesians 6:12)

---

[1] The Abel and Harlow Child Molestation Prevention Study; childmolestationprevention.org

DEMONSTRATING A LIVING CHURCH IN A DYING CULTURE

By Anita McCoy

"Keep hope alive." These words, perhaps spoken many times in a variety of settings, were first delivered to the American people in a compelling speech given at the 1988 Democratic National Convention where a contender announced that his name would go into nomination for the Presidency of the United States of America. Instantly, these three simple words became a *social anthem* of American culture. People across this nation were inspired to find their own voice of influence and as musical bands, songs, and projects emerged, messages of hope reignited a people desperate for change and renewal. KEEP HOPE ALIVE! So profound is the collective meaning of these words that from the twentieth century to the twenty-first century, there is not a living soul that would argue the relevance and power of hope and its ability to make hearts come alive.

The Power of Influence

Religion, among the Seven Mountains, has an extraordinary influence upon society. Webster's Dictionary defines influence as: "the capacity to have an effect on the character, development, or behavior of someone or something." Through influence, an individual or group affects the character or behavior of others and thereby develops and advances a particular culture. E.B. Taylor, an eighteenth-century English anthropologist, was the first to coin the term *culture*. He discovered that culture and society go together because the study of society is incomplete without the proper understanding of culture. Specifically, E. B. Taylor defined culture as: "that complex whole which includes knowledge, belief, art, morals, law, custom, and any other capabilities and habits acquired by man as a member of society." All of society has a heart that beats to a specific rhythm of cultural expression, resulting in a distinct sound. Understanding this, I believe it's quite natural to expect the Church to influence and improve society through one of the richest virtues known to man, the virtue of hope. Christ's Church in the Mountain of Religion is a unique and authentic culture designed and influenced by God to restore hope and manifest His Kingdom here on Earth.

God's Kingdom Culture

The Church empowered by the Spirit of God is to influence and advance all the other cultural expressions within the Seven Mountains. Hence, Revelation 11:15 makes this declaration, *"The Kingdoms of this world are to become the Kingdoms of our Lord, and of his Christ; and He shall reign forever..."* God spared no creativity or ingenuity in fashioning His *Design of Influence*. In Genesis 1:26, God the Father, the CEO of Heaven said to His Board of Directors, the Word (Jesus), the Holy Spirit, and Himself, *"Let Us make man in our image, after our likeness: and let them have dominion."* Each director purposed to honor this vision, giving themselves completely and employing their heavenly attributes to ensure that at the appointed time, a model would emerge to influence the Earth.

What are these Heavenly Attributes?

There are distinct qualities and attributes that authenticate a culture. What gives a culture its greatest impact, is the soundness of its character and the thrust of its language. Character is developed through introspection, and discipline establishes our values. An article written by the group Language and Culture Worldwide, states this about language: "The languages we speak provide us with the words and concepts to describe the world around us, allowing us to verbalize certain values easily. Anything we as a cultural group value will surely have a known and easily understandable term." What this confirms for us is the reality that every culture has its own distinct language. When Christ arrived on the scene, He announced, *"The Kingdom of Heaven is at hand."* The Apostle Paul later taught the Church that *"the Kingdom of God is not meat and drink; but righteousness and peace, and joy in the Holy Ghost"* (Romans 14:17). So, two things are established: 1) the Kingdom of Heaven is easily accessible to us because Christ came into the world; and 2) the Holy Spirit's attributes of righteousness, peace, and joy validate you as a representative of the Kingdom of Heaven! Further substantiating this truth, the Apostle Peter expresses that this *lively hope* has been given through the resurrection of Jesus, and the inheritance, power and unspeakable joy therein contained, must exude from the life of every believer, which collectively forms His Church!

The Dilemma

My conviction is that the Church exists to compel society to discover its common virtues and support a corporate expression of shared values that will ultimately alter society as a whole. In order for this to happen, the Church must rediscover and embrace its virtue, immerse itself fully in the power of the Holy Spirit, and authenticate *a Kingdom language* that will influence communities, cities, and nations to turn from the kingdoms of this world (system) to the Kingdom of God. The dilemma is, *a house divided against itself cannot stand*. But sadly, in the twenty-first century, there are far too many instances where the Church is divided by denominationalism, racism, socialism, sexism, and many other expressions of culturalism. Hence, our character and language are infected and the influence of our God-given purpose is neutralized.

A House Divided

We are living in a society in which the influence of the Church culture is dying. What seems to be killing the influence of the Church is the Church itself. In my limited research, I saw two things; a disheartening decline in the Christian faith, and the negative impact of denominations among Christians. A review of the 2014 Religious Landscape Study, conducted June 4 - September 20, 2014 from the Pew Research Center, revealed that while "the United States remains home to more Christians than any other country in the world, the percentage of adults (ages 18 and older) who describe themselves as Christians had a massive drop from 78.4% in 2007 to 70.6% in 2014. Over the same period, Americans describing themselves as atheists, agnostic, or "nothing in particular" jumped more than six points, from 16.1% to 22.8%." This dilemma is further compounded by Christians that are separated into an estimated 41,000 denominations—divisions arising due to doctrinal differences between Christian groups.

In Matthew 12: 25, Jesus displayed His Kingdom authority to heal one possessed with the devil and the religious leaders (the Pharisees) accused him of operating under the power of Satan. As He spoke to them, Jesus addressed the impact of division and He wasn't casual about it. Jesus, knowing their divisive thoughts, said, *"Every Kingdom divided against itself is brought to desolation, and every city or house divided against itself will not stand."* I believe we can learn something more from this. As the Church, we must cleave to the truths of the Word of God and leave every tradition and doctrinal belief that promotes *division* in place of *Kingdom*. We must realize that in order to influence the world and see transformation, we must separate from cultural belief systems that promote conformity to the world and be agents of change.

In this twenty-first century, we are witnessing a rapid cultural decline; an erosion of morals, values, and ethics; a disregard for human life; a perversion of truth; and increasing evil in the land. It is time for the Church to lay down its differences and arise as the Body of Christ to manifest the same Kingdom authority Jesus modeled. We must fully receive the person of the Holy Spirit, that third, powerful member of the Godhead. As revealed in John 20: 21-22, while visiting the disciples after His crucifixion, Jesus says, *"Peace be unto you: as my Father hath sent me, even so send I you. And when he had said this, he breathed on them, and saith unto them, Receive ye the Holy Ghost."*

Personal Encounters with the Holy Spirit

I was born in the middle of the twenty-first century (1963), a decade shaken by social issues that had national and global impact. A "counterculture" emerged in the 60s, finding expression among the Civil Rights Movement,

Gay Rights Movement, a second wave of the feminist movement, and an anti-war movement. It displayed the sense of dissatisfaction that was widespread in America and across the globe.

My mother, a young woman in her 20's, was right in the middle of this movement. Being a single parent of two very young children, she could have joined the bandwagon of any one of the platforms erected during this time period, but *something* got a hold of her! My mother, through the influence of another Spirit-filled believer, had a born-again encounter, giving her life to Jesus in July 1964. And as the story goes, three weeks later, she was radically transformed when she received the baptism of the Holy Spirit, with the evidence of speaking in other tongues. My mother was instantly empowered to preach, teach, and prophesy, and as she did, the sick were healed, the bound were delivered, and souls were influenced by the power of God.

Altered at the Altar

My mother's conversion soon gave way to my own encounter with the power of God as one of the cultural changes with my mother resulted in her taking me to the Friday *All-night prayer meetings*. Instead of watching the Worldwide Wrestling Federation at home, I watched children and adults wrestle in prayer at the altar!

There was something special about midnight, the hour of *breakthrough*! It was one of those moments, a Friday night at midnight that I, only four years old, received the baptism of the Holy Ghost! Over the years, I discovered that this encounter opened the door to other operations of the supernatural power of God manifesting to advance the Kingdom of God!

As Jesus said unto the disciples, I say unto you, *"Behold, the Kingdom of Heaven is at hand...receive ye the Holy Ghost!"*

Declarative Prayer Points

1. I declare the Spirit of repentance upon the Church (Joel 2:12-14; Deuteronomy 4:29).
2. I declare the Spirit of humility is changing my heart and renewing my spirit (Psalm 51).

3. I declare that the Church is one even as God and Jesus are one (John 17:23).
4. I declare as the Church unifies, the power of the Gospel will influence the world (John 17:20-21).
5. I declare the heavens are open and times of refreshing are blowing over the Church (Acts 3:19).
6. I declare the winds of change are blowing, releasing fresh moves of the Holy Spirit (Acts 2:17-21).
7. I declare revival is in the land, souls are being saved, and disciples are made daily (Matt. 28:18-20).
8. 8, I declare that love is the cultural expression and language of my life and the Church (Matt. 14:14).
9. Spirits of religion and traditions are disrupted and power is restored to the Church (Luke 11:14-28).
10. I declare every system is shaking as the Church moves out in authority and boldness (Acts 4:31-33).

---

[1] http://www.washingtontimes.com/blog/watercooler/2012/dec/23/84-percent-world-population-has-faith-third-are-ch/

[2] http://www.pewforum.org/.

[3] https://en.wikipedia.org/wiki/Counterculture_of_the_1960s

[4] www.preservearticles.com/201101173455/characteristics-of-culture.html

[5] https://en.wikipedia.org/wiki/Culture

[6] http://www.americanrhetoric.com/speeches/jessejackson1988dnc.htm

[7] www.languageandculture.com/cultures-languages

[8] http://www.yourarticlelibrary.com/culture/culture-the-meaning-characteristics-and-functions/9577/ 3rd definition on culture.

[9] http://www.pewforum.org/2015/05/12/americas-changing-religious-landscape/

[10] https://en.wikipedia.org/wiki/List_of_Christian_denominations

WHERE ARE MY PRIESTS?

By Adrienne Sumler

A Call Back To Priestly Worship

In 20 years of ministry, over 17 years of pastoring that transitioned into an Apostolic call on my life, I have been charged to seek out the Holy Spirit concerning the heart of God and true worship. The Lord spoke to me saying that He did not just want to visit, but dwell among His people. "I want you to build a habitation in the Church and in the people." He then began to give me greater revelation about the Levitical Priesthood and then the Prophet Amos' prophecy in Amos 9:11.

As the Holy Spirit continued to lead us as a local church in a new direction, just as He did King David, we evolved into a corporate body of worshippers releasing a Davidic Sound. As we continued consecrating and entering into His presence, God spoke to me again, but not as a statement rather a question—*Where are my priests?*

Gods and Nations

In my opinion, the Mountain of Religion is the most important of the seven mountains because of freewill; you first have to choose what God you will serve while you are alive. I remember as a new believer, when people spoke about God, I would assume they would be speaking about the Lord Jesus Christ, and soon discovered they were speaking of many other gods. God has said from the beginning, "Thou shall not have no other gods before me."

In 20 years of leading the people of God in worship, I've discovered something; an age-old battle over who we worship and who receives our worship. As an apostle who has invaded this mountain, these are things we need to be aware of to effectively fight on this mountain.

Apostle Paula states, "Apostleship always hinges upon two immutable things; gods and nations. Nations belonging to gods and apostles as their dispatched representatives or ambassadors are sent to deliver or return a nation to the god that birthed or won it in combat. Immutable means unchanging over time or unable to be changed; or not capable of or susceptible to change." We are called to subdue and conquer every false god that does not bow to the name of Jesus Christ, and to lead ALL nations to the Lord by effectively fighting on this mountain.

Facing other gods on the Mountain

First, let's define *religion*. It refers to the "service and worship of God or the supernatural (other spirits, gods, and deities; emphasis added); commitment or devotion to religious faith or observance."

A popular belief in the twentieth century is that religion is about our observances. In addition to observances, we talk about denominations, rituals, and our faith. Nothing could be further from the truth. When we look at God's constant disappointment with Israel, it originates with the worship of other gods. From Genesis, in creation, Adam and Eve entertained false gods (Genesis 3:5). In Exodus 20:1-3, God wrote in the Ten Commandments, "Thou shalt have no other gods before me," but on getting to Exodus 32:1-6, the Israelites were once again worshipping false gods (the golden calf).

This biblical pattern and battle is evident from Genesis to Revelation. Who will you choose to worship? Jesus encountered this same problem with the Pharisees in Mark 7:7-9.

So, in Psalms 82, God establishes, "I am God in the sanctuary and I judge among all the gods." And in the book of Isaiah 45:5; 43:11, He says, "I am the lord, and there is none else, there is no God beside me... He is the only true GOD and besides him there is no other." God has spoken of how jealous He is over His creation, and on the Mountain of Religion, any other god, spirit, or deity is counterfeit and trespassing. God made the Heavens and the Earth and has given it to the children of men (Genesis 1:1, 2; Psalm 115:16). It has no legal right to reside or function on that mountain. So in prayer, we have the power and authority to annihilate anything that's not like God on that mountain.

We can't give away what rightfully and indiscriminately belongs to Him by design, that is, *Our Worship*. It is a sin to worship or serve anything or anyone other than Him. He is jealous over what rightfully belongs to Him as creator God. Our wholehearted worship is His and His alone.

The Synagogues vs. the Temple

As previously stated, God asked, "Where are my priests?" So let's understand who priests were, their roles, duties, and functions. Priest in Hebrew is "Kohen," meaning one who offers sacrifices, one authorized to perform the sacred rites of a religion, especially as a mediatory agent between humans and God. In the office of a priest, one became a ritual expert and obtained special knowledge of the techniques of worship. He was also accepted as the religious spiritual leader in which they spent their lives teaching others about their religion.

Under the New Testament covenant, we are all called to be Kings and Priests (Revelation 1:6; 2:9) set apart by Father God for His purposes. All priests were Levites, but not all Levites were priests. Aaron, Moses' brother, was a High Priest and called at Mount Sinai (Exodus 28:1) and the High Priest had different qualifications, roles, and duties as opposed to the priest. Future priests had to be descendants of Aaron out of his lineage (Exodus 28:1, 44; 30:30; 40:13-15). Furthermore, only those designated for priestly or High Priest duties could perform them. Listed below are some of the priest and High Priest duties and functions. However this is not an exhaustive list.

Priestly Duties and Functions

1. To teach the people
2. To keep the Tabernacle in order

3. To keep the Tabernacle pure, and the people in purity
4. To serve as judges, to judge between clean and unclean, and holy and unholy.

The High Priest's Duties and Functions

1. He was the supreme leader over the priest.
2. He also could have no bodily defects and had to be holy in conduct.
3. He was called to inquire of the Lord about individual or national issues.
4. He was the only one who would lead sacrifices on the Day of Atonement.
5. Only the High Priest could wear the Urim and the Thummin (engraved, dice-like stones used to determine truth or falsity).The people would go to know the will of God (Numbers 27:21). In the New Testament, there is a reference to the High Priest as having the gift of prophecy (John 11:49-52).

Lastly, the Lord told Aaron as the High Priest, "You shall have no inheritance in their land, nor shall you have any portion among them; **I am your portion and your inheritance** among the children of Israel" (emphasis mine).

He was all they needed as they performed the work of the Lord. God Himself would provide and called them to:

1. Keep the Temple holy and pure
2. Watch over the Temple
3. Protect God's Presence
4. Worship God in His dwelling and habitation where His glory rests for eternity
5. Never let the fire of God go out in the Temple.

Our responsibility as the New Creation, New Covenant Church is to return to priestly worship. As Apostles, Prophets (Ephesians 3:20), and Pastors, our role is to legislate what comes in and out of the house of God. There is a regional assignment that Jesus has released to the Ecclesia. We have governmental jurisdictional authority over these regions and our churches to help us govern the body of Christ. So let's talk about the Non-Priests.

In 586 BC, the Temple was destroyed and the population was carried off in captivity (2 Kings 25:1-21). They began to meet in groups and meetings because the Temple was no more (Jeremiah 34:1-7). The Prophets gave warnings, but they were not heeded. They could not do sacrifices but fellowship, informal prayer, and study.

Temple worship and spiritual life fell to a record low, and open idolatry was being practiced throughout the land. By the time the Temple was rebuilt, and sacrificial worship restored under the Levitical priesthood, the prototype of the Temple was replaced with Synagogue Worship. The Church had become institutionalized.

The Pharisees found themselves in leading positions in synagogues springing up everywhere, and the Pharisees had become advocates of excessive legalism, pride of position, and scriptural error (Matthew 23:1-39; Mark 7:1-13).

Lastly, Priestly Worship consists of sacrifices and intercession unto God while Synagogal Worship promotes prayer, study, and fellowship. Temple Priests were expected to work in the "Shechinah," in the Hebrew "Shekinah" (the dwelling/settling presence of God's glory). The Rabbis and Pharisees were not.

The Bible is silent when it comes to whether God endorsed synagogues but Jesus and His disciples went to them on the Sabbath (Luke 4:16; Acts 17:1-3; Acts 18:1-4). But they were ministering, not receiving. The Temple priests would close the Temple to attend synagogues. So now we understand why God posed the question to me, "Where are my priests?" He wants us, as modern-day priests, to restore priestly worship and to be walking, living, dwelling places for His glory. He wants us as conduits of heavenly worship.

Declarations and Decrees

1. Father, we declare every believer on this mountain will love you and be made in your image daily (Genesis 1:26; John 14:15).
2. We declare, Father, your people will return to you, and worship you in spirit and in truth on this mountain (1 John 4:23, 24).
3. We declare the Spirit of God is rising and moving and we no longer have fear to fight (2 Timothy 1:7; 1 John 4:18).
4. Father, release the Host of Heaven to fight for and defend your ecclesia (Psalm 68:17).

Prayer

Father, we are sons and heirs to the Kingdom. We are seated in Heavenly places in Christ Jesus, far above principalities, powers and spiritual wickedness in high places. We are your stratospheric Warriors co-laboring in Kingdom Advancement. We ask that you give us unique battle plans, blueprints, and strategies to build for you. We ask the precious Holy Spirit to lead, empower, and guide us. We thank you for new realms of power and authority. Angels are destroying and chasing the enemy on your behalf. Release the Host of Heaven on our behalf. We thank you that true Praise and Worship is being restored and we love you for it in Jesus' name.

Amen.

[1] Hendrickson (July) The Holy Bible King James Version (Sixth Printing). Publishers Edition MA, Peabody

[2] Price, A. Paula (2005) Eternity's Generals: The Wisdom of Apostleship. An Essential Guide & Comprehensive Tool for Contemporary Apostles. Tulsa, OK: Flaming Vision Publications

[3] The Three-In- One Concise Bible Reference Companion, (1982) Nashville, TN Thomas Nelson Publishers God pg.291

[4] (n.d.) In Dictionary.com Retrieved October 10, 2017 from http://www.dictionary.com/browse/god

[5] (n.d.) Easton Bible Dictionary Retrieved October 9, 2017 from http://www.bilestudytools.com/dictionary/priest

[6] (n.d.) Merriam Webster Dictionary Retrieved October 9, 2017 from http://meriam-webster.com/dictionary/priest

[7] Old Testament Priest and Priesthood, 2017 Retrieved from http://www.biblecharts.orgoldtestament/oldtestamentpriestandpriesthood.pdf

[8] Encyclopedia Britannica Retrieved October 12, 2017 from http://www.brittaica.com/topic/priest-Christianity

[9] In Wikipedia. Priest. (2017). En.m.wikipedia.org. Retrieved October 12, 2017 from http://en.m.wikipedia.org/wiki/Priest

[10] Worship, (2017). A LEVITICAL CALL TO MODERN DAY WORSHIP// David Carnine. Nextgen Blog Retrieved October 12, 2017 from http://blog.nextgenworship.com/blog-post?post=levitical-call-to-worship

[11] "What was the biblical role of the high priest?" (2017). Got Questions Retrieved October 12, 2017 from http://www.gotquestions.org/high-priest.html

[12] Rudolph, M. (2012) A Call to Priestly Worship. Retrieved from http://www.genesisobservatory.us/onev/Documents/Papers/Call%to%20Priestly%20Worship.pdf

INFLUENCE OF THE NEW AGE MOVEMENT IN THE CHURCH

By Roseline Keni

Introduction

From its very conception and appellation, the New Age movement was based on a lie, especially the notion that it offers something new to a world that always aggravates towards something recent and fresh. It is strange that this religious movement has the word "New" to its name, despite the fact that its foundation is based on ancient religions. It therefore makes sense to uncover and pinpoint its very central motive, which is basically to challenge the power and authority of Jehovah, the sovereign God, and most especially the birth, life, death, and resurrection of Jesus. Of course, the New Age is demonically orchestrated to deceive God's people, especially those who are ignorant about God's Word. But we thank God for the Holy Spirit, our Teacher who helps us not to be ignorant of the devices of the enemy.

> *"My people are destroyed for lack of knowledge"* (Hosea 4:6 KJV).

When God's people are detached and do not know what is right or true, they end up being ruined. The spirit of religion, in its capacity as a major curse and stronghold in the Church today, presents itself as a formidable obstacle to the flow and move of God and the revelation of the love and lordship of Jesus Christ over His Church. We can all agree that God's truth is found in His Word and His righteousness is found in intimacy with Him through the fellowship of His Spirit, the blood of His Son, and the transforming power of His Word. From this standpoint, we can therefore conclude that it is because Christians do not study the Word of God nor develop an intimate relationship with the Lord, that causes them to be easily swept away by any form of New Age doctrine.

New Age is based on astrology and is a mixture of Eastern religious practices and metaphysical thought systems. It also constitutes different theologies, moral diversity, philosophy, and nature. According to Rapidnet.com, the New Age Movement is grounded in Eastern mystical religion comprising of Taoism, Buddhism, Western Occultism, but mainly Hinduism. The New Age Movement is vast in its practices and it is sociological, spiritual, and ideological in its philosophy. These multi-facet and multi-focused aspects have contributed to its easy access and deception in the Church.

History and Definition of New Age Movement

The Aquarius Age is what is termed "The New Age," as everything is new in the way the world system is supposed to function. It is an age of a more egalitarian lifestyle which believes that we are all gods and therefore have the right to do as we please. So we can clearly see that it is all about power and that sounds very familiar to what took place in the Garden of Eden, *"And a tree desirable to make one wise, she took of its fruit and ate"* (Genesis 3:6).

New Age Practices that are Being Performed in the Church

> *"Dear friends, do not believe every spirit, but test the spirits to see whether they are from God, because many false prophets have gone out into the world"* (1 John 4:1).

This scripture comes to mind when the Church of God copies practices from the world or other religions without testing the spirit or their biblical implication. The following practices have been adopted by the Church without testing the spirit or the source:

Universalism

The New Age Movement believes in universal views and they believe that evil does not exist. The religion is founded on principles that there is nothing like judgment and therefore, hell does not exist and everyone in the end, winds up in a good place. This is contrary to Scripture since the Bible is very specific about the existence of Heaven and hell and judgment occurring after death. Although this belief is so contrary to Scripture, some Christians are starting to believe this deception.

> *"And as it is appointed unto men once to die, but after this the judgment"* (Hebrews 9:27).

According to a magazine titled *Jesus Will Save You—Whether You Agree or Not* on belief.net, Carlton Pearson who is the founder of the Azusa Interdenominational Fellowship of Christian Churches and the pastor of Higher Dimensions Family Church in Oklahoma, holds a controversial belief that no matter one's belief or religion, we will all end up in Heaven because Jesus Christ already died to redeem the whole world and there is nothing else left to be done.

Many Christians are being corrupted with lies that come with being opened to different religious practices that promise to bring in universal love and unity, whereas the Bible clearly speaks of us being united with brothers in the Lord and not in different religions.

Female Deities/Astrology

Although occult practices that include the worship of female deity have long been practiced by Catholicism in the worship of Mary, they are beginning to creep into the body of Christ due to the New Age movement. Christians are also starting to get into giving a word of knowledge based not on what the Lord is telling them, but what they are picking up as the aura from the person, whereas the word of knowledge is supernatural knowledge about an incident that is presently happening in that person's life or a past event.

Relativism

A foundational belief of New Agers is that of relativism and the Church has delved into this in an attempt to improve evangelistic strategies. The whole theory of relativism is the belief system that everything is based on how we feel; something is good if it makes us feel good, and bad if it makes us feel bad. So we now have Christians who determine what is good by whether it makes them feel good or not.

Karma

Another New Age belief system that I have heard Christians talk about is "karma." According to an article titled *Christian Karma* on the Bethel Christian Church website, it is written that karma has crept into the churches with Christians thinking that one's present life is a result of what they have done in the past. Although the Bible talks about sowing and reaping, it also states that *"If anyone wishes to come after Me, he must deny himself, and take up his cross daily and follow Me" (Luke 9:23).* So, Christians have to know that the Lord requires us to deny ourselves and follow Him, and that might entail bearing persecution and trials and dying to self and worldly pleasure.

My Personal Experience with New Age

My experience with New Age came when I was searching for deliverance ministries for my son who was diagnosed with autism when he was 22 months old. I contacted a woman who had a testimony of delivering a girl with very low functioning autism on her website and she was more than happy to take us through the process. She did a session with me and another with my husband and then the following sessions started to be a bit scary, as she asked me to renounce speaking in tongues because she believes it opens the door to the enemy in my family. She asked me to confess and repent from using anointing oil and attending any Pentecostal Church services because they were rooted in idolatry. That caused me to withdraw from her, but she wouldn't let go and kept sending me emails about how her spirit guide told her that my son is not yet healed because deep inside me, I wish he was dead and I have released a spirit of death onto my son. She also stated that the Lord is not pleased with me, since I have decided to let my son suffer because I wanted to continue speaking in tongues and practicing Pentecostalism as she believes there are no gifts of the Spirit. I knew she was into something funny when she kept referring to her spirit guides helping her and telling her these things about us. I stopped picking up her calls and responding to her emails, and my husband and I prayed and disconnected ourselves from her. We had to war in the spirit intensely to break everything off of us that resulted from our connection with her.

Declarations to Break Free From the New Age Stronghold

> *"Wherefore come out from among them, and be ye separate, says the Lord, and touch not the unclean thing; and I will receive you"* (2 Corinthians 6:17).

If you were involved in New Age or any other occult movements,

1) Ask the Lord to forgive you like you would do any other sin; ask Him to cleanse you with His blood and set you free from any demonic entanglements. *"For all have sinned, and come short of the glory of God"* (Romans 3:23).

2) List all the occult/New Age practices you have been involved in and then renounce them one after the other by praying like this:

   A. I repent and renounce my involvement in ----------New Age/occult practice and Lord, please forgive me.
   B. I blot out any occult image that was imprinted on my body or that I traced on someone else's body, with the fire of the Holy Ghost and by the blood of the Lamb.

3) Call out the names of each symbol as you renounce them one after the other.

I denounce and reject all symbols of the occult as well as geometry that were used on me for physical or emotional healing. *"And by His stripes we are healed"* (Isaiah 53:5).

In Jesus' name, I release the fire of the Holy Ghost to consume any keys/symbols used on me to create pathway for "energy" and "higher mind" and awaken my "third eye."

I plead the blood of Jesus over my mind and cancel any prayer that was done to awaken my emotions and consciousness.

4) Go around areas in your home or office and pray and renounce these practices and also collect any item (clothing, jewelry, and literature paraphernalia) connected to the occult and create a pile and burn them.

5) Pray and ask the Holy Ghost to lead you to a Spirit-led/prophetic Church and make this your new spiritual family.

6) Sever all ties with people from the New Age/occult group. *"Wherefore come out from among them, and be ye separate, saith the Lord, and touch not the unclean thing; and I will receive you"* (2 Corinthians 6:17).

---

[1] http://www.rapidnet.com/~jbeard/bdm/Cults/newage.htm

[2] http://www.beliefnet.com/faiths/2003/06/jesus-will-save-you-whether-you-agree-or-not.aspx#Dsdc0USQFkkzSDEl.99

[3] https://www.merriam-webster.com/dictionary/karma

[4] https://bethelchapelchurch.com/christian-karma/

[5] https://isaiahministries.wordpress.com/2014/11/27/martial-arts-yoga-does-it-have-any-place-in-the-church/

SOUNDING THE TRUMPET OF AWAKENING IN THE NEW SEASON OF REVIVAL

By Thapelo Kgabage

The book of Ecclesiastes 1:4 (KJV) highlights to us that God continuously raises a generation after another in fulfillment of His mandate upon the face of the Earth. *"[One] generation passeth away, and [another] generation cometh: but the earth abideth for ever."*

Initially, when God created man in His image, He gave them dominion over the Earth. This shows that from the beginning, God created man as the most influential being that has been placed upon the face of the Earth. And it happened in the Garden of Eden that man lost what God gave him, that is dominion, but thank God today, He has restored it unto man through His Son Jesus Christ (Genesis 3).

Today, many in the Church still fail to comprehend and believe that God has restored unto us the authority and power to subdue and to have dominion in this present world, not in the future, but now, through His Great Commission (Matthew 28:19-20). It doesn't matter whether the past generation failed to live to God's ordained standards, their time has passed and now it is time for this rising generation to do God's business. One generation passes away, and another generation comes (Ecclesiastes 1:4), and God wants His Church (Ekklesia – the called out), in this present generation, to influence the world in all spheres of life.

There is an evil that is happening under the sun today. It is seen as an error which proceeded from many church leaders, and has been going on for years and years. It is now bound to change in this season, through this generation. That is, the Church has been influenced too much by the world instead of being the greatest influence on it. The songs they sing, the dance, and even setups in many places of worship, including their teachings, are purely influenced by the outside world. It is a serious error that needs to be corrected (Ecclesiastes 10:5-7). It is of a concern that many in the Church of God have taken a turn for the worse, departing from God's principles and surrendering to false, senseless, unscriptural, and deceptive teaching that glorifies men and promotes worldly behavior.

The Lord, in this prophetic and apostolic season of reformation, is ready and already has raised a new breed, a generation of generals in His army, ready to influence and impact the world with the true Gospel of the Heavenly Kingdom. God calls them the *agents of change*, the true Kingdom ambassadors. This is the generation that is ready to influence the world and its governmental systems, and instill heavenly systems, influencing man's cultural systems and beliefs by instilling the Kingdom culture and changing the traditions of mankind that make the Word of God to be of non-effect across the whole world. The time for change is not tomorrow, but now. The long-awaited season is now, the long-awaited generation that has been prophesied beforehand is here—His current Church.

Our age is questionable to many, like that of Gideon whom God used in bringing down the altars of the false god Baal; asking themselves, "How will this young generation make it?" Our stature, like that of young David when facing giant Goliath, is of doubt to many, but through us, God is ready once more to bring down and cut off the head of wicked spiritual giants of the world and bring peace and stability to His Church and the world as a whole.

This is the generation that has the solution to the current evil world, and God is ready to turn tables around in the present world system through us. This is the generation that did not send themselves to the world, but they have been commissioned from above to represent Christ while ministering in power and authority. They're ambassadors of the Kingdom of God and not their own kingdoms like others did in their generations.

That is the biggest problem and danger to any generation; seeking self-glory and building kingdoms for themselves. This can destroy the generation, thus it is paramount that a generation draws men to God instead of themselves. God hates sharing His glory and being replaced by His creation. Many have deviated from teaching the truths of God's Word and taken God completely out of the whole picture. Instead, they are leading people astray with their false teachings from seducing demons and devils, and God wants to correct such in this season. This current generation is one that believes God and His Word, and understands that God's Word is the standard and it is final.

It is the appointed time by the Lord to raise story-changers who, with the truth in their mouth, shall correct the deceptive teachings of the world that have crept into the Church. They will remove the veil from the eyes of God's people, including non-believers in the world, so that they can see the truths of God. It is the generation with opened eyes, open understanding, and opened scriptures. It is time the truth—which is the Word of God, grows mightily in our cities and prevails in the whole world.

God needs the generation that shall occupy, and not only to occupy, but also do His business until He comes again, and God says that you are that generation.

Many are asking about this generation, "Who are they? Where has it been all along and where is it going?" This is the same Kingdom people you see daily on the streets and in our local churches, looking like the nobodies, whom the world doesn't even recognize. Some of their names are unknown, yet the Lord is working in them, mentoring them for times such as this, with the fresh message directly from the Throne of Grace. They are the people of the Throne with great influence and impact.

This is the generation with a voice of victory, the generation that shall shout victory upon the face of the Earth and it shall be, and it shall shout with a loud anointed voice of authority, power, and grace. This is the generation that speaks directly to the realms of the spirit and makes changes to spiritual climates through the authority vested in them. Someone might ask, "Where is that generation that has been spoken of?" God says, "It is here and you are that generation."

Prophetic Declarations and Prayer Points for our Generation

1. I am born of God, and I overcome the world (1 John 5:4).
2. I am the light of the world (Matthew 5:14).
3. I am a Kingdom ambassador (2 Corinthians 5:20).
4. I am the chosen generation (1 Peter 2:9).
5. I am the salt of the Earth (Matthew 5:13).
6. Christ is in me, the Hope of Glory (Colossian 1:27).
7. I was born and separated to impact many nations of the world, and many shall come to the light through me and my descendants (Genesis 15:14-17).
8. The life of God flows in me (1 John 5:12).
9. I was born to impact and change lives and am a crown of God's beauty to display His Glory (Isaiah 62:1-3).
10. I am a testimony to the whole world (Revelation 12:11).

SPIRITUAL SONSHIP

By Alandis Porter

Have you ever wondered what our lives and the world would be like if Adam and Eve had never disobeyed God?

The Beginning - Genesis 1:26-27 KJV

[26] And God said, Let us make man in our image, after our likeness: and let them have dominion over the fish of the sea, and over the fowl of the air, and over the cattle, and over all the earth, and over every creeping thing that creepeth upon the earth. [27] So God created man in his own image, in the image of God created he him; male and female created he them.

God put all that He was in man. Man housed the DNA OF GOD (Divine Nature of the Almighty), His character, His love, and His creativity. God then gave man dominion over the Earth.

As we read the creation account of mankind in Genesis, we find that man had even been given the power in His mouth to name, create, and cultivate, like God. He was perfect in nature and had perfect and uninterrupted fellowship with God; the perfect father-son relationship. This was the perfect prototype of what God wants with us today. But for us to truly become and live as sons, we must first know and understand the design and relationship before us.

The Original

God gave man dominion (Genesis 1:28-30), but He also gave him one specific instruction; not to eat of the tree of the knowledge of good and evil (Genesis 2:16-17.) He wanted His creation to understand that, "Yes, you are designed in my image and house my power but you are not equal with me!" Well, the devil in the serpent knew this, and decided, "I'm doomed for eternity, so why not play on the compassion of the woman and get her to seduce this man, Adam, to eat of the tree?"

This leads us to...

The Fall (Genesis 3:1-6)

Man and woman, who had the perfect setup in Eden, with a perfect relationship with God, now had disobeyed the one thing they were instructed not to do. This caused not just an enlightenment God did not want them to have, but also a separation from Him. They were banished from the garden, and that separation from God brought an orphan spirit onto the Earth. (An orphan spirit brings a sense of abandonment, loneliness, alienation, and isolation.) Almost immediately after the fall in Eden, the fruit of this orphan spirit was passed on to the offspring of Adam and Eve, culminating in Cain murdering his brother, Abel, because of jealousy when God the Father didn't accept Cain's offering.

The Effects

To make matters worse, in contemporary society, with the breakup of the nuclear family, large amounts of people are not only alienated from God, but are brought up without the loving care and security of their biological fathers. Man lost his place because of one act of disobedience. It has affected every facet of the family unit.

I have also been affected by this plight in being disconnected from my own father all my life. This is becoming more common than not in society.

Child Abandonment

Over 400,000,000 abandoned children live on their own on the streets of hundreds of cities around the world.

- *Every 2 seconds, a child becomes an orphan.*
- *1,000,000,000 of the world's families live on less than a dollar a day.*

- *Authorities estimate that child pornography is a $20 billion a year industry; too many abandoned children end up as victims of this deviant activity.*
- *UNICEF estimates that nearly 1,000,000 children enter the sex trade every year.*
- *According to the World Health Organization, malnutrition is the single biggest contributor to child mortality rates worldwide.*
- *Many street children use a number of inhalants (glue, gasoline, lighter fluid) and illegal drugs (marijuana, cocaine, and heroin).*

United States Divorce Statistics

Most people already know that around 50 percent of marriages in the United States end in divorce. The number is similarly high in many other developed nations.

When you break that down by number of marriages:
41 percent of first marriages end in divorce.
60 percent of second marriages end in divorce.
73 percent of third marriages end in divorce.

These are just a few of the issues that the fall brought through the ages of time and still continue. The only way this could be stopped and broken is by us accepting God's love for us, which He proved before we even knew Him. The Father sacrificed everything by giving His son in our place. He gave a blueprint of what love looks like, acts like, and talks like. He gave all! No man, dead or alive, has sacrificed as much.

Restoration (John 3:16)

God yet loved man even though he disobeyed and sinned. God found a way to bring man back into the right relationship and give back to him the image, authority, and sonship He started with. God wanted His original plan completed. He wanted us to experience the Hebrew definition of "son"—a household of life!

Ephesians 1:6-7 KJV
[6] To the praise of the glory of his grace, wherein he hath made us accepted in the beloved. [7] In whom we have redemption through his

blood, the forgiveness of sins, according to the riches of his grace;

This is now our heritage and birthright. We can never walk in the power and authority God has given us if we don't have a revelation of who He is and who we are in Him (Galatians 2:20).

This is what the enemy never wants us to accept and know because it knows that many strongholds will be broken and families restored. Men will take their rightful place again in the home, naturally and spiritually leading the family as in the beginning like Adam.

We must take our place as the Kingdom Ambassadors God ordained us to be! We must take our marriages back, our sons and daughters back, by breaking the chains and filling our hearts and minds with the truth again, and letting love lead again. We must let God have first place again!

Declarations (Our inheritance as sons and daughters)

1. I declare I have been made a son, and all orphan traits are far from me.
2. I am an heir of God and joint heirs with Jesus by the blood.
3. I have the DNA of God and Love is my reflection.
4. I am the heritage of the Lord, and all the generations that follow are His kinship.
5. I commit my family to the Lord, and declare to be filled with love and governed by peace.
6. My life is governed by the voice of my Father and a stranger I do not follow.
7. I decree that God is the head of my family and we respond in love in every situation.
8. When I encounter the unexpected, I allow God's word to be my roadmap.
9. I declare I speak only what God my Father speaks and no idle words are in my vocabulary.
10. I declare I am a stranger to failure but a vehicle of success!

Prayer

Father, we thank you for the sacrifice that you made in the Son even though the disobedience from Adam and Eve brought much despair. You loved us and made a way to restore us back to the status of sons and daughters of the Kingdom of Light!

We pray over all sons, daughters, and the families affected by the fall. We pray that those that have not yet come to know you will have a God-encounter that will change their life and the life of their families. We come against every stronghold that has been attached to bloodlines. We come against abandonment and alienation. We come against an orphan mentality; we come against the spirit of suicide and the fear of not being good enough. We appropriate the blood to every void left by sin. We cover our families today under your protection. Father, we apply the blood to our bloodlines back a thousand years. We decree and declare our loved ones will hunger and thirst for you, Lord. We speak and we say, you are the God of our children and you govern our every move. We thank you in advance for those you've chosen to lead, who will carry truth to those lost and broken by sin; they will teach, train, and mentor them. They will be patient with them and fight with them until they see deliverance. Thank you, Father, for making us whole again and restoring us back to the place you destined us to be. We decree and declare we shall remain planted in your house to see your goodness for the rest of our days. In Jesus' name we pray. Amen!

---

[1] All Scripture from The Kings James version Bible

[2] The Huffington Post/THE BLOG

America's Abandoned Children

05/26/2011 03:04 pm ET Updated Jul 25, 2011

[3] McKinley Irvin/ FAMILY LAW BLOG

32 SHOCKING DIVORCE STATISTICS

Oct 30, 2012 12:00am PD

[4] Mike Connell/The Orphan Spirit

Sun 16 Jan 2011

CHAPTER 6

THE MOUNTAIN OF BUSINESS

Business is God's idea. Prosperity is God's idea. The Bible is full of entrepreneurs. The Mountain of Government should provide a just and fair-level playing field for those on the Mountain of Business to prosper. Unfortunately, as on the Government Mountain, there is the possibility for much greed and corruption on this mountain, as dark forces of Mammon seek to control and oppress many through those individuals doing business without a conscience. This is where a righteous government must protect the most vulnerable in society such as the poor, orphans, widows, and the fatherless. Scripture is very clear about that with many references. Not to do so is an injustice.

We saw this in the US economic crash of 2008, where Wall Street bankers full of greed almost destroyed the economy, and then made a deal with the government to bail them out after millions of Americans lost homes and retirement accounts. Then after getting bailed out, they rewarded themselves with lavish bonuses. Those on the top of this mountain have the potential to destroy a nation. Righteous business leaders on the top of this mountain have the potential to bless a nation, and even break the power of systemic poverty. Transformed business leaders will transform this mountain, speaking truth to business and modeling what prosperous Kingdom businesses should look like.

THE TIME TO START YOUR BUSINESS—IS NOW!

By Yolanda Mosby

According to Fortune.com, "Everyone knows that running a business isn't cheap." I beg to differ with this statement, because nowadays, there are so many different ways to start up a business with little or no cost. Besides, the Word of God says, "But thou shalt remember the Lord thy God; for it is He that giveth thee power to get wealth…" (Deuteronomy 8:18 KJV)

Operating a business can be run from your hand and lap, simply by the touch of a button from your smartphone and/or laptop computer. With the current advanced technology we have today, one can launch and operate their business by internet through a smartphone, iPad, or just by making a phone call to retailers and placing an order.

God reminds us in 3 John 2, *"Beloved, I wish above all things that thou mayest prosper and be in health, even as thy soul prospereth."* The Spirit of the LORD is saying He has ordained our prosperity to be ongoing, although there may be a waiting season before we continue to work on things that must be completed. This is why we must write the vision and make it plain upon tables (paper), that *"he may run that readeth it"* (Habakkuk 2:2). The written vision is like a blueprint for our business. Habakkuk 2:3 says, *"For the vision is yet for an appointed time;"* therefore, it's important to write the vision when the Spirit of the LORD reveals it to you. *"But at the end it shall speak and not lie; though it tarry, wait for it: because it will surely come, it will not tarry."*

My Journey

In the year of 2001, just after moving to Jacksonville, Florida, I found myself searching for employment, which led me to The Potter's House Christian Academy as an after-school teacher. Although I found employment, something was missing.

After receiving that wonderful job, I later found out that I no longer had childcare for my son, Mark. After searching for childcare relentlessly, I cried out to God and made my request known unto Him. I asked God to provide me with the career that would allow me to care for my family and bring home a steady income. God honored my request!

One beautiful day, I took a ride to the Naval Air Station, Jacksonville. While driving by the Child Development Center, there was a sign that read, "Child Development Home Providers are needed." Wow! To my surprise, this was God's way of answering my prayers. This was an opportunity that would allow me to own a business and work from home while providing care for other children and families who were in need of childcare. What had initially seemed to be a bad situation in my life actually turned out to be a blessing. I learned even in that hard place that we must cry out to God because He promised to hear us when we cry out to Him. After signing up to become an In-Home family childcare provider, I found my purpose by caring for children in my home. God allowed me to open my home as a business owner, while providing a safe, loving, and caring environment for many children who were in need of childcare.

This opportunity was just what God had planned for me for the future. I paid a minimum out-of-pocket fee because the U.S. Navy sponsored all trainings and supplies; therefore, God allowed my needs of childcare to reveal the gifts and talents that I never knew I had. Being without childcare allowed me to tap into the hidden gifts God had placed within me. I hereby advise that even in the midst of your hard times, please take an opportunity to cry out to God…and may He answer your cry according to His will in Jesus' Name.

10 Steps to Start Your Business

1. **Conduct Market Research.**

Market research will tell you if there's an opportunity to turn your idea into a successful business. It's a way to gather information about potential customers and businesses already operating in your area. Use that information to find a competitive advantage for your business.

2. **Write Your Business Plan.**

Your business plan is the foundation of your business. It's a roadmap for how to structure, run, and grow your business. You'll use it to convince people that working with you or investing in your company is a smart choice.

3. **Fund Your Business.**

Your business plan will help figure out how much money you'll need to start your business. If you don't have that amount at hand, you'll need to either raise or borrow the capital. Fortunately, there are more ways than ever to find the capital you need.

4. **Pick Your Business Location.**

Your business location is one of the most important decisions you'll make. Whether you're setting up a brick-and-mortar business, or launching an online store, the choice you make could affect your taxes, legal requirements, and revenue.

5. **Choose a Business Structure.**

The legal structure you choose for your business will impact your business registration requirements, how much you pay in taxes, and your personal liability.

6. **Choose Your Business' Name.**

It's not easy to pick the perfect name. You'll want one that reflects your brand and captures your spirit. You'll also want to make sure that your business name isn't already being used by someone else.

7. **Register Your Business.**

Once you've picked the perfect business name, it's time to make it legal and protect your brand. If you're doing business under a name different than your own, you'll need to register with the federal government, and maybe your state government as well.

8. Get Federal and Tax IDs.

You'll use your employer identification number (EIN) for important steps to start and grow your business, like opening a bank account and paying taxes. It's a social security number for your business. Some — but not all — states require you to get a tax ID as well.

9. Apply for Licenses and Permits.

Keep your business running smoothly by staying legally compliant. The licenses and permits you need for your business will vary by industry, state, location, and other factors.

10. Open a business bank account.

A small business checking account can help you handle legal, tax, and day-to-day issues. The good news is it's easy to set one up if you have the right registrations and paperwork.

Congratulations! It's time to cut the big ribbon. Your business is officially open. Now focus on managing and growing your business (source: *sba.gov*).

Decrees & Declarations

1. I am made in the image and after the likeness of God.
2. I bind the spirit of procrastination. I will prosper in my businesses as God has ordained for me to do so.
3. I will start my business and employ many people.
4. I decree my business will help the economy grow strong.
5. I decree my business will be a continued and ongoing marketplace ministry for others and myself.
6. I decree local, state, government, and international contracts in favor with God.
7. I decree a dominion mindset that the hidden treasures of God shall be revealed to me that will cause me to prosper in my businesses.
8. I decree that the right people will enter my life that will cause me to follow the paths God has ordained for my life and businesses.

All Scriptures are from the King James Bible

WEALTH CREATION FOR KINGDOM ADVANCEMENT

By Amanda Samuels

What Every Believer Needs to Know

When the Lord instructed me to write a book addressing one of the seven mountains of cultural influence, January 12, 2017, during a period of fasting and prayer, I knew it was not just another book, but a message He wanted me to urgently convey to His Church. The world is rapidly advancing. However, the body of Christ is yet to lead in righteousness, justice, power, and innovation. Among the many issues affecting believers, poverty ranks very high and has been a stumbling block to the Church fulfilling its mandate. It is a fact that poverty affects people of every age, gender, religion, or culture, but what is heart-breaking is that many believers live below their potential and are unable to fulfill their assignment due to lack of resources. In writing this chapter, I aim not to establish a doctrine that salvation is merely to make every believer rich. Rather, I want to remind you that Christ's work of redemption empowers us as Kingdom citizens to walk in victory and fulfill our preordained destiny. Permit me to highlight some startling facts pertaining to poverty among the Christian community as I raise awareness and present solutions to an issue we all must play a role in solving.

A Cause for Concern

A study conducted in 2016, by World Bank reveals, "Despite decades of substantial progress in boosting prosperity and reducing poverty, the world continues to suffer from substantial inequalities. For example, the poorest children are four times less likely than the richest children to be enrolled in primary education across developing countries. Among the estimated 780 million illiterate adults worldwide, nearly two-thirds are women. Poor people face higher risks of malnutrition and death in childhood and lower odds of receiving key health care interventions. Such inequalities are associated with high financial cost, affect economic growth, and generate social and political burdens and barriers."

According to a new Pew Research Center demographics analysis, "Christians remained the largest religious group in the world in 2015, making up nearly a third (31%) of Earth's 7.3 billion people."

A recent research and analysis as part of a collaboration between the Guyana Budget & Policy Institute and the Center for New Economic Studies shows, "The level of poverty and associated levels of malnourishment will have dire consequences on the future health of the population and the potential for future economic growth in Guyana unless immediate steps are taken to address these issues. More than 36 percent of Guyanese or almost 4 in 10 people are living in poverty i.e. surviving on an income of U$1.75 per day or G$10,494 per month, according to the Guyana Poverty Reduction Strategy: 2011 – 2015.[1] Further, 19 percent of Guyanese or almost 2 in 10 people are living in extreme poverty i.e. surviving on an income of U$1.25 per day or G$7,550 per month.[2] People living in poverty simply do not have sufficient income to pay for enough food to meet daily caloric and nutrition intake required for proper nourishment and healthy and productive lives." If these statistics are not a cause for concern to the Church, then we are asleep.

Born for More

I've discovered that many Christians who attend regular weekly services and faithfully support the work of the Lord with their tithes and offerings, still experience financial bondage. This is not to say that their actions are wrong. What is lacking is the understanding of biblical prosperity and financial stewardship. As a young, Afro-Guyanese woman, who spent most of my life in a religious environment, I was among the number of believers who lived below their potential. This was largely due to a lack of knowledge of my identity and purpose. As I grew in my relationship with God, I discovered my purpose and was able to maximize my potential. Every believer has an assignment to fulfill. When God created the human race, He gave us dominion over the Earth. We were made in the image and likeness of God. As Kingdom citizens, we possess power and authority to manifest Heaven's realities on Earth through our words. We have the ability to create. Proverbs 18:21 declares, "Death and life are in the power of the tongue, and those who love it will eat its fruit." What we release from our lips will become a reality. Speak the Word of the Lord to the mountain of business and see the economic systems of this world come into alignment with the will of God.

Creating Wealth—Impacting Culture

God desires for us to prosper. According to Deuteronomy 8:18, He has given us the power to create wealth. Over the years, the enemy has used many false teachings to: (1) keep believers in bondage, and (2) hinder the Church from fulfilling purpose. Sadly, some Christians believe that wealth is a sign of compromise and poverty is a mark of humility.

In Matthew chapter 25, Jesus used the parable of the talents to encourage believers to be good stewards of the gifts and talents He has given us. The Church is the agent of the Kingdom of God and the pillar of truth. The Apostle Paul in his letter to the assembly at Ephesus, admonished the leaders to equip the saints for the work of ministry. This instruction from Christ is still applicable to the twenty-first-century Church.

The body of Christ should be taught the biblical principles of wealth creation, financial stewardship, and giving. This will cause the yoke of poverty to be broken and believers will be able walk in victory and fulfill their assignment. Wealth creation is a solution to many of the challenges experienced by believers and those in the world. Like Joseph and countless other marketplace leaders, we are called to impact those around us through divine wisdom and creative ideas in business. Believers are the salt and light of the Earth.

As we go forth and fulfill our assignments in righteousness, power, and authority, darkness will be exposed and ethics and morality will be restored. Martin Luther King Jr. said, "Darkness cannot drive out darkness: only light can do that. Hate cannot drive out hate: only love can do that." Christ's resurrection and ascension assures us that the Church is undefeated. We are a victorious people. Jesus said, "…I will build my church, and the gates of hades shall not prevail against it" (Matthew 16: 18). Proverbs 31:16-20 speaks of a glorious church impacting culture by investing in profitable business ventures and living a lifestyle of generosity. As marketplace leaders, our assignments are important for the advancement of the Kingdom. From a position of authority and victory, let's go forth and scale the Mountain of Business.

Prayer

Father, I thank you that I am made in your image and likeness. According to Psalm 24:1, "The Earth is the Lord's, and all its fullness, the world and those who dwell therein." I declare that creation is ready to receive my gifts and Kingdom mandate as a child of the Most High God. As a business leader, I am equipped and empowered to fulfill my assignment with integrity and excellence. I declare that I am free from fear and every yoke/limitation of the enemy. Today, I receive vision, grace, and anointing to manifest Heaven's realities on Earth. I possess divine wisdom and knowledge which give me a competitive advantage in the marketplace. I am clothed with favor and strength and will impact every person I am called to serve. I walk in faith, hope, and love and leave a legacy of godliness for generations to follow. By the grace and power of God, I overcome every challenge or obstacle in my path. I declare that the eternal purposes of God for my life and business are established on Earth as in Heaven, in the mighty name of Jesus, amen.

Prophetic Decrees & Declarations

1. I decree righteousness and justice will prevail in my nation, region, and the nations of the world (Proverbs 14:34 KJB).
2. I decree peace, economic growth, and development in every nation

(Jeremiah 29: 4-7 & 1Timothy 2:1-6 NKJV).

3. I receive divine wisdom and knowledge of witty inventions (Proverbs 8:12 KJB).
4. I walk in great faith and strength for Kingdom exploits (Daniel 11:32 KJB).
5. I receive divine connections, influence, and uncommon favor with God and man (Luke 2:52 KJB).
6. I declare that the works of my hands are blessed (Deuteronomy 28:12 KJB).
7. I decree fruitfulness, exponential business growth, and high rate of returns for my investment (Psalms 1:1-3 KJB).
8. I declare that the purposes of the Lord for my life and business shall prevail (Proverbs 19:21 ISV).
9. I declare that the plans of the enemy for my life and business shall not prosper (Isaiah 54:17 KJB).
10. I decree abundant blessings over my team, customers, suppliers, and investors (Genesis 12:3 KJB).

---

[1] World Bank Group. (2016, October). Poverty and Shared Prosperity 2016. Retrieved from
https://openknowledge.worldbank.org/bitstream/handle/10986/25078/9781464809583.pdf

[2] Pew Research Center. (2017, April). Christians remain world's largest religious group, but they are declining in Europe. Retrieved from http://www.pewresearch.org/fact-tank/2017/04/05/christians-remain-worlds-largest-religious-group-but-they-are-declining-in-europe/

[3] Guyana Budget & Policy Institute. (2017, August). Poverty Facts: Almost 4 in 10 Guyanese Cannot Afford Basic Costs of Living. Retrieved from
http://gbpi.institute/2017/08/27/poverty-facts-almost-4-in-10-guyanese-cannot-afford-basic-costs-of-living/

[4] Index Mundi. (2016, July). Guyana Demographics Profile 2017. Retrieved from
http://www.indexmundi.com/guyana/demographics_profile.html

THE SUPERNATURAL DIMENSION OF THE APOSTOLIC ENTREPRENEUR

By Jonelle Maxwell

Question—What if I told you miracles are supposed to follow you as an Entrepreneur? Well, the answer is YES! Many believers have settled with just being a business owner without ever truly walking out their God-given assignment as an Apostolic Entrepreneur. In this hour, God is revealing new dynamics and releasing blueprints on how to do business HIS WAY. This is the only way we will be able to see the Kingdom of God on the mountain of business in the massive ingathering of souls, and the great wealth transfer. God is sending laborers because surely the harvest is plentiful. Are you willing to go outside of the four walls to win the masses? Well, if you are, then let's go on a little journey in how to win souls with Jesus!

As you read, these are blueprints and strategies from the Courtroom of Heaven. God began to reveal these things to me as I walked through the trenches of the true mantle of an Apostolic Entrepreneur. These experiences are not references from a book—ONLY THROUGH THE POWER OF THE HOLY SPIRIT! While you are reading, you will receive an impartation and activation. I pray that new realms of the Apostolic Entrepreneur Dimension begin to open, and that you receive a new wave of revelatory insight. God is taking us into the supernatural dimension to bring forth what He and He alone desires to come forth through His Ecclesia. So, let's press past all of the ideology and get on the path to host His Glory on the mountain of business.

Understanding the Apostolic Entrepreneur

I am going to give you some, but not limited to, clarity within the Apostolic mantle. First, let's start by defining the word Apostolic. The Apostolic is God's Government. It is the expressed image of Christ operating through the Ecclesia on Earth. We have been translated into His Government, which is the Kingdom of God, not only to speak the language but to become the language.

Who hath delivered us from the power of darkness, And hath TRANSLATED us into the Kingdom of His dear Son.
(Colossians 1:13 KJV)

Now, let's define the term Entrepreneur. Entrepreneur is more than just a business owner. An Entrepreneur is an establisher of businesses that have been innovated through blueprints, strategies, creativity, and new paradigm shifts to accommodate the era in which we now live in today. The Entrepreneur must stay on the cutting edge of the business mountain to remain relevant. Therefore, having an Apostolic mantle will allow the Entrepreneur to operate in the full measure of grace, and maximize the sphere of influence to the highest potential.

The Commissioning of the Apostolic Entrepreneur

When God prepares the Apostolic Entrepreneur, He first solidifies the call by giving the vision to see the outcome BEFORE the pioneering even begins. Having a God-given vision is very important, especially when times get tough, you will be strong enough to not give up. You must know without a shadow of a doubt, that God commissioned you with this kind of assignment. Also, know who you are in Him and who He is in you (1 John 4:4). Let me encourage you; if God called you to it, He will most definitely get you through it. You are more than able to possess the land! So, do not allow fear, doubt, unbelief, the naysayers, the devil, and even yourself, get in the way of the mandate God has assigned to you. There are GREAT REWARDS awaiting those that obey God!

The Ability to Create: Your Region Needs What You Have

God has given us the creative ability to create, develop, design, innovate, and birth new inventions (Proverbs 8:12). Also, God will allow His Entrepreneurs to see a need coming and then give strategies to meet those needs. This is what separates your business from all the rest. Believers must come away from duplicating the world's model of how we should do things. God has His own system which is His Kingdom and that's the way it has always been from the very beginning (Genesis 1:1).

Apostolic Team

Next, you cannot accomplish the mandate on your own. The assignment of the team is to establish God's Government on Earth together. We see this method being demonstrated with Jesus and His disciples. Now, if Jesus understood this method of needing a team, then what about us? Jesus chose twelve disciples to reproduce Himself. Why did He choose twelve? Well, the number twelve means government, which is the representation of the mantle you carry as an Apostolic Entrepreneur. So can you see the vision? Jesus called the disciples together. Then, he empowered them by imparting in them what He had. Lastly, He commissioned them with an assignment (John 9:1; 2).

Tap Into Supernatural Wealth: Net Pay

Every Apostolic Entrepreneur has wealth assigned to their mantle. But how exactly do we unlock this realm? Easy. Have you ever heard the phrase, "find your niche"? You know that one thing that will make your business *POP*. This kind of method is found in Luke 5:4-11. The disciples had been tolling all night and they caught absolutely nothing—UNTIL Jesus spoke and gave instructions. Due to their obedience to the *rhema word*, they had so much that the net broke. God wants you to have so much that you will need assistance to bring in the harvest! When was the last time you went to Jesus about your business? He has the answer that will cause your business to be the head and not the tail. We will be above only, and not beneath, if we put His Kingdom first (Matthew 6:33). This will happen as we maintain our focus on the King and the Kingdom. The

Supernatural Realm of Wealth will always be at our disposal. GLORY! Are you excited yet? Well, I am!

Build, Build, and Rebuild Again: Repairer of the Breach

Your people will rebuild the ancient ruins and will raise up the age-old foundations; you will be called Repairer of Broken Walls, Restorer of Streets with Dwellings.(Isaiah 58:12 NIV)

Lastly, after you have tapped into the Supernatural Wealth Realm, it is time to build and rebuild. The Apostolic realm has a building anointing that comes with blueprints and solutions. This is when God gives you solutions for your assigned region or regions to solve problems. God wants you to rebuild the city. This too is one of the mandates of the Apostolic Entrepreneur. Do you know what your region has need of? Do you know what they struggle with the most? These are things you should know because this is key in what kind of service you should offer your region. You are there to serve your region! Remember all needs are not the same for every region, so your relationship with the Holy Spirit is always going to be maintained so He can show you.

Another thing to remember, you cannot do anything without Him. This method will cause you to become the "solution" for your region and everyone will come to seek you out for answers. All you need is one opportunity to solve a problem and your name will be spread abroad! We also see this demonstrated with Solomon. The Queen of Sheba HEARD about his wisdom and came looking for him, bringing wealth with her (I. Kings 10:1-29). The ONLY way this method is truly going to work for you is if you start getting out there in the community; BEFORE building, learn your assigned region and the people. Allow the Holy Spirit to make you visual. You will be surprised how people will start communicating with you about the cries of the city. Remain open and ready because the solutions to their cry will start to flow from the Holy Spirit when you least expect it.

Prayer, Decrees and Declarations

Father God, I thank you for the mantle of an Apostolic Entrepreneur. I thank you that you have entrusted me with the assignment to establish your government on the Mountain of Business that souls will be drawn to you. Your Word declares to let our light so shine before men that they may see our good works and glorify the Father who is in Heaven, according to Matthew 5:16. So, Father be glorified in me and through me.

1. I decree and declare that it is not by might, nor by power, but it is by your Spirit.

   Zechariah 4:6.

2. I decree and declare that you have given me the spirit of wisdom and revelation in the knowledge of you, according to Ephesians 1:17.
3. I decree and declare the eyes of my understanding is being enlightened for the assignment in the marketplace that you have given me even before the foundations of the Earth, according to Ephesians 1:18.
4. I decree and declare that I will remember that it is you, Lord God, that has given me the power to possess and acquire wealth to establish your covenant, according to Deuteronomy 8:18.
5. I decree and declare that I receive new witty inventions for my marketplace assignment, according to Proverbs 8:16.
6. I decree and declare that I am rich in every area of business because your WORD declares that the blessing of the Lord makes rich, and adds no sorrow to it, according to Proverbs 10:22.
7. I decree and declare that I am the head and not the tail; above only, and not beneath, according to Deuteronomy 28:13.
8. I decree and declare that the Lord causes all grace to abound towards me in all things and at all times. I am abounding in every good work, according to 2 Corinthians 9:8.
9. I decree and declare the Lord is taking pleasure in prospering me in my business, according to Psalms 35:27.
10. I decree and declare that I NOW arise, shine, for your light has come, and the glory of the LORD rises upon me, according to Isaiah 60:1.

11. I decree and declare that though darkness covers the Earth and thick darkness is over the peoples, the LORD rises upon me and His glory appears over me, according to Isaiah 60:2
12. I decree and declare that the nations are coming to the light of Christ that is in me, and kings to the brightness of my dawning, according to Isaiah 60:3.
13. I decree and declare that assistance is coming to rebuild the walls of this region with me, according to Isaiah 60:12.

---

[1] http://www.bibleprophecytruth.com/topics/bible-numbers

[2] https://www.kingjamesbibleonline.org/

INFLUENCE ON THE BUSINESS MOUNTAIN

By Carla Wallace

Moving into the place of influence in the marketplace takes favor, humility, strategies, Kingdom principles, and wisdom from God. There are many ways to scale the Mountain of Business, but God's way is preeminent. As a Kingdom believer, our goals should be: being fruitful, multiplying, subduing the Earth, and replenishing it with Kingdom culture believers to help sustain and take dominion on the Mountain of Business. In Genesis, God commanded Adam and Eve (Genesis 1:28) as well as Noah (Genesis 9:1) on fruitfulness, multiplying, subduing, and taking dominion.

The Hidden Agendas

It is imperative that Kingdom Business Owners and Kingdom Executives begin to arise and scale the Mountain of Business. As corporate America pushes their agenda to influence the culture, we as Kingdom believers need to push the Kingdom of God's agenda to influence our home, communities, cities, regions, and nation. In an article by Glenn Llopis, he expressed his concerns regarding Americans' enterprise future, based on his conversations with Fortune 500 leaders. In those major corporations, hidden agendas and true intentions were not exposed to the ones who were executing the corporate strategies (Forbes, Glenn Llopis).

Fortune 500 leaders' hidden agendas disrupt business growth and leadership within the company. They also impact the culture of our workplace and society. Imagine working for a company who promotes something that appears to be positive from the outside but the true agenda is to have a negative impact on society. This impact may directly affect the consumer or indirectly targets another audience through byproducts or resources.

As an executive, you will encounter sensitive information before it is put into action. During this time-period, you have the advantage to speak against and or pray against the negative hidden agenda that your corporation will release to their consumers or employees. Proverbs 12:22 talks about lying lips and how the Lord takes delight in those who deal truthfully. Speaking the truth may not always be easy but standing for what is right will be the most rewarding for you, the company, and your subordinates. When Joseph was working in Potiphar's house, his decision to have integrity cost him something. It cost him his freedom and he was sent to prison but meanwhile, in prison, he met the Pharaoh's chief cup-bearer, who brought his name up before the King (Genesis 40).

Moving into the Place of Influence

I started my career as an Entrepreneur and then later went from Licensed Vocational Nurse to a Registered Nurse. I still maintain business ownership, while being a nurse because I believe in multi-streams of income. While working as an LVN, I encountered many people with higher authority that did not have integrity. I remember thinking within me that, when I obtain a position of influence, I would maintain integrity and work for the betterment of the lives of our patients, families, co-workers, and companies, while bringing Kingdom people into position to help transform the way companies conduct business. Colossians 3:23 references that we should work with our heart and not for men. When I began working from my heart with the heart of Christ, God began to show favor toward me, with men.

Even though I was working and serving in the *pit*, I was found to be faithful to my beliefs and work. I was able to go in and obtain positions that I didn't even qualify for and was able to do what God had called me to do for that season. For each career move, I began asking God, "What is my assignment here?" I began to dismantle things that were not of God and was able to push Kingdom agenda in the positions I held. Even when I was working, but feeling trapped in a prison, I continued to hire, train, and show the love of Christ. And one day, someone remembered my name, which took me to a higher position to dismantle things within a region and to promote the Kingdom agenda on the next level in the palace.

Joseph was successful in the pit, prison, and palace. His gifting in administration and his character placed him before influential men. As second-in-command in Egypt, he was able to effect godly change in the nation as well as execute on initiatives that would save many other nations from destitution. In the same manner, moving up in corporate America can provide you with many opportunities to execute Kingdom initiatives that will produce good fruit on the mountain of business. This effect can be greatly multiplied by hiring, training, and equipping your employees to work in a manner that honors God and advances the Kingdom.

Declaration and Prayer Points

1. I will be set in influential positions and will observe and do what God has commanded me to do (Deuteronomy 28:1).
2. I am blessed to be a blessing to others in my home, in my job, in my community, and to those who I'm specifically assigned to in the marketplace (Deuteronomy 28:2-6).
3. As I move up in position, I will be found trustworthy and qualified to the vision of the Kingdom of God as I operate in the business world and marketplace (2 Timothy 3:1-7).
4. I will operate and will be the example that will inspire those underneath me and those above me to create an atmosphere of peace. I will effectively use my power and influence to benefit the expansion of the Kingdom (1 Peter 5:3).
5. I will obtain the skills necessary to take a leadership position in higher places within a corporation or business (1 Chronicles 15:22).
6. I will be filled with the Spirit of God, and will lead with wisdom, understanding, and knowledge in all business and work dealings

(Exodus 31:3).
7. I will walk with integrity and in uprightness in all that I do (1 Kings 9:4).
8. I will be fruitful, I will multiply, I will replenish, and I will subdue in every sphere and environment I am called to (Genesis 1:28).
9. I will have wisdom like Solomon and gifts and favor like Joseph to consult those who are in key positions (1 Kings 4:34).

Prayer and Decree

Father in the name of Jesus, I come thanking you for all that you have done for me. I thank you in advance for what you are about to do in my life. I bless your mighty name, for you are the King of kings and the ruler of all things. Lord, I asked that you give me favor with men, to place me in a key position to rule and take dominion in the business world. Give me wisdom like Solomon to be able to have men sit and to listen to the divine solutions that you have given me for corporate and business issues and systems' problems. Father, expand my thinking to encompass divine wisdom for strategic decision-making. Lord, allow me to perform with the spirit of excellence and be successful on any level like Joseph. Let me rule with humility, allow me to prosper in the thing that will give your name the glory and honor. Father, allow the Holy Spirit to lead and guide me on my assignments. I command every spirit that comes against my elevation into key positions to be annihilated. I decree and declare that the Lord will establish the works of my hands in Jesus' name. Amen (Genesis 41:40, Psalms 90:17).

---

[1] Glenn Llopis (2011, Nov) https://www.forbes.com/sites/glennllopis/2011/11/07/objectives-define-intentions-why-leaders-must-reveal-their-hidden-agendas/#6dc6ae816cd4

[2] By Jean; http://www.lifebydesignco.com/3-ways-to-do-ministry-in-the-marketplace

[3] Needle, David (2004). *Business in Context: An Introduction to Business and Its Environment.* ISBN 978-1861529923.

ECONOMICS FOR THE GOOD SEED

By Shevon L. Sampson

In 1993, I sat in a small church in California and watched many churchgoers cry and plead with God for physical and financial help. Sunday after Sunday, I sat and pondered how many of them were overlooking their God-given gifts and talents. I could not help but wonder how many entrepreneurs, landlords, CEOs, and millionaires were in the room. More importantly, I wondered how many Kingdom entrepreneurs, landlords, CEOs, and millionaires were in the room! The more I sat there, the louder I could hear the Lord say, "Do business until I return!" Now I must ask you: Are you doing business until He returns? What are you doing as you wait for the glorious re-entry of the King of kings and Lord of lords?

There are two financial realms in constant operation: the world's economic system and God's economic system.

The world's monetary framework has three central focuses partitioned by economic classes (Payne, 1995):

1. Generational Poverty. Those in generational poverty focus on survival, relationships, and entertainment.
2. Middle Class. The middle class focuses on work and achievement.
3. Wealthy. The wealthy focus on social, political, and financial connections.

The world's financial framework constructs its esteems in light of insatiability and self-centeredness. People pay little mind to who gets hurt while asking, "How do I get as much as I can?" The world's framework sees cash as the journey's end instead of a vehicle to advance the Kingdom.

In contrast to the world's economic system, the Kingdom system doesn't have classes. There is no generational poverty in Heaven's economy. Your faith determines success and advancement, and your stewardship and seed sowing determine prosperity.

You have a choice. You can strive for temporary earthly economic gain, or you can lay up your treasures in heaven. Matthew 6:19-21 (NKJV) tells us:

> *Do not lay up for yourselves treasures on earth, where moth*
> *and rust destroy and where thieves break in and steal;*
> *but lay up for yourselves treasures in heaven, where neither*
> *moth nor rust destroys and where thieves do not break in and steal.*
> *For where your treasure is, there your heart will be also.*

Having your treasures in Heaven sounds better, doesn't it? After all, Heaven is eternal and Earth is temporal. But *how* do you lay up treasures in Heaven? Romans 12:6 tells us to use the talents that God gave us. Luke 12:48 says that to whom much is given, much is required, which means that the more God gives you in talent, skill, and material things, the more He expects you to use them to lead souls to Him and perform good works so that people see Jesus when they look at you. That is *how* you lay up treasures in Heaven. There is no heavenly reward for climbing the corporate ladder and stepping on people as you go.

Both the world's system and God's system have their masters, and it is impossible to serve both! It doesn't matter who you are or what kind of business you run; you can only serve one master. The Bible puts it this way:

> *"No one can serve two masters; for either he will hate the one*
> *and love the other, or else he will be loyal to the one*
> *and despise the other. You cannot serve God and mammon."*
> Matthew 6:24 (NKJV)

Serving mammon by worshiping riches will influence your pursuits and push you to acquire and hold onto things. You will become weary under the burden of debt (Pope, 2007).

It is a hard decision to make, but you must choose whom you will serve. Joshua 24:15 (NKJV) says, *"As for me and my house, we will serve the Lord."*

Pick a master and pick a day to start. I remember when I first decided that I would make God my Master and be a sower of seed for the Kingdom. At first, the thought of sowing my talents, resources, and especially my time, seemed unfruitful and counterproductive to the demands of life that towered over me. But I did it anyway and invested time to learn more about the biblical sowing and reaping. I set aside a portion of my resources and exercised my faith. I reaped a bountiful harvest that could not be explained in man's vernacular. The heavenly economy went to work on behalf of my faith, and I give God the glory.

God's economy is an on-time economy. He shows up with the blessings you need when you need them, and in ways you won't believe until you experience them. That doesn't happen with the world's economy.

I recall a specific instance when I was buying a house. I made the down payment and funded Escrow and thought I was all set. Then the realtor dropped a bombshell: I needed $10,000 for *reserves*. Where would it come from? I had no more reserves to give.

I was under God's economy, and He was my Master, so I didn't need any reserves. You see, God owns the cattle on a thousand hills (Psalm 50:10), the Earth is the Lord's and the fullness thereof (Psalm 24:1), and nothing is too hard for God (Jeremiah 32:27). What happened next cemented my faith in Kingdom economics. A woman walked up to me out of the blue and said, "I heard you need $10,000. Follow me to the bank, and I will give you what you need." And she did! Just like that. I know who told her what I needed, and I give Him the glory for proving to me that His way works.

What a triumphant day it is when it sinks into your spirit that if you choose God as your Master, He takes a personal interest in everything about your life. Psalm 139 says that He knows everything about you. Matthew 6:8 says He knows every need *before* you ask, and Luke 12:7 assures you that He even knows every hair on your head.

Everything you have comes from God. When you choose God's economy, you get the privilege of being God's distributor, and you get to disperse His resources where He tells you to. That makes you an entrepreneur for the Kingdom!

It is my prayer that we all make a conscious effort to debunk from mammon and make a genuine decision to choose God as our Master, which is a decision that can be seen more than heard. So, join me in asking the Holy Spirit to guide us into all truth (John 16:13) as we make up our minds to be the good seed and Kingdom distributors after His heart!

Declaration & Decree

Lord, we come boldly to your throne, and we decree and declare that none of our sisters and brothers in the marketplace are submitting to mammon. We declare we are delivered from ungodly partnerships and alliances.

According to Ephesian 5:11, we expose darkness in the marketplace and replace it with Kingdom standards. We bind fear and intimidation, and loose power, love, and sound minds, according to 2 Timothy 1:17.

We declare and command the enemy to loosen his grips and let our sisters and brothers in the marketplace freely step into their God-given assignment, excel, and be salt and light in their areas of influence. We pray according to Genesis 12:2 and declare that you, oh God, have made us a great nation and have blessed us to be a blessing, even in the marketplace.

We believe you, Father, for Spirit-led vision, and according to Habakkuk 2:2, we are writing the visions down and making them plain. We declare that we know that you, Jehovah, are our only God and we walk in your image and likeness (Genesis 1:27).

We decree and declare that we can exercise the authority and dominion of King Jesus in the marketplace. Let signs and wonders follow as we impact culture as Kingdom children in business and all other areas of influence. We declare that as we scale the mountain of the marketplace. May the Lord's favor blanket and surround us like a shield.

We declare and decree that the wealth of the wicked is no longer being stored, but it is released to the good seeds who are the sons and daughters of the Kingdom. We receive the mind of Christ (I Corinthians 2:16) and the wisdom of God (James 3:17) as we do business, buy, sell, lead, and distribute on Earth.

Father, according to John 10:27, we hear your Voice, and the voice of strangers we do not follow. We declare that as your wealth is released, we hear clearly where to distribute your resources. We receive both finances and uncommon favor from the north, south, east, and west for the advancing of your Kingdom, and it is so, in the matchless name of King Yeshua.

---

[1] Payne, R. K. (1995). A Framework: Understanding and Working with Students and Adults from Poverty. Baytown, TX: RFT Pub.

[2] Pope, E. (2007). The Two Economies: God's vs. World. Retrieved August 19, 2017, from http://www.foundationsforliving.org/articles/foundation/twoeconomies.html

CHAPTER 7

THE MOUNTAIN OF GOVERNMENT

The Mountain of Government, as the delegated authority, must through the rule of law, provide a framework of justice and freedom, and create an environment of peace and safety in which sustainable prosperity can become the goal for all people. The decrees and laws of this mountain can and will affect all the other mountains. The ruler on this mountain must govern with integrity and justice. Many developing nations have incredible natural resources, but extremely impoverished people. One of the primary reasons is *bad leaders* and *bad rules* creating an environment of terrible corruption where only a very small percentage prospers, primarily through nepotism. Proverbs 29:2 says that when the righteous are in authority, people rejoice, but when the wicked man rules, people groan.

For many years, there was an attitude in the Church that government or politics was dirty business, and any believers who got involved would get dirty. So the Church abdicated their responsibility here and let the wicked govern. What a terrible error in judgment! The Scriptures give us great examples of those called to influence government, such as Daniel, Joseph, Esther, Deborah, along with many others. Righteous leaders that are called to government must reclaim this mountain.

UNITED NATIONS A GATEWAY INTO GLOBAL REFORMATION

By Michelle Brown

Kingdom Influencers in Government Arise

We're living in a time where God is raising up a new breed of believers that He is strategically positioning within the Mountain of Government that will have great political power and worldly influence. These Kingdom influencers will bring in a movement of change that will help usher in God's glorious Kingdom here on Earth. This new movement is bold, innovative, and powerful, and it will shift old paradigms that in times past have limited God from moving freely. It will aid God in fulfilling His ultimate goal to establish world peace, by influencing legislature, shaping and molding policy and social reform into a Kingdom culture. The United Nations is a hub and gateway to the nations of the world and will help bridge the gap where religion has created a wedge.

When we look at the definition of a *king* in the marketplace, it is a leader of great wealth and/or major influence. As a "king's heart is in the hand of the Lord, like the rivers of water; He turns it wherever He wishes" (Proverbs 21:1, NKJV), God will use believers to touch the heart of kings within government and the United Nations, thus, allowing them to have favor with them. They will be people of authority, who walk in dominion and use the name of Jesus as a weapon to gain influence and carry out their mandate. Whether these believers are senior leaders or janitors, they can be used by God. As the Word of God states, "...at the name of Jesus every knee should bow..." (Philippians 2:10, KJV), so there is tremendous power in the name of Jesus.

Also, Rich Marshall states, *"The authority God has given you is a weapon to enable you to fulfill His purposes, and bring about His destiny in your life. Use your authority as a weapon for Him."* By rising up in power as a child of God, and releasing the name of Jesus in the atmosphere in a low whisper under your breath, or meditating on it, will allow things to supernaturally line up. I have done this countless times in the marketplace and have seen the manifestation of God's word and my prophetic declarations.

Favor with Great Kings and Kingdoms

Queen Esther came at a time when the Jewish people faced execution by the government and God mandated her to fast and pray for them so the plans of the enemy would be destroyed. When her uncle Mordecai saw her hesitation, he said, "...who knows whether you have not come to the kingdom for such a time as this?" (Esther 4:14, ESV). So, it was apparent that God had purposely placed her there at that particular time. After following God's instructions, she developed a boldness and asked the King if he could spare her lineage. Because she was obedient, God gave her favor with the King, where he granted her request.

Similarly, the Lord supernaturally placed Joseph into positions within *Kairos* timing where he had favor with kings, government officials and world leaders. To that effect, God allowed him to move up in rank from what we would consider one of the lowest levels as a prisoner, to eventually becoming a *king* and head of his government. Our obedience to our assignment not only prepares us, but also unlocks our destiny to divinely connect with *kings* or transition into that headship role, where we'll be able to impact governments and shift nations on a much greater scale.

World Leaders of Integrity

Corruption in government is at an all-time high and God wants Kings with integrity to occupy positions of power and authority. Looking at the days of Moses where he served as a King, the Lord led him to choose leaders that were honorable, and these were "capable, honest men who fear God and hate bribes" (Exodus 18:21, NLT); they were chosen to help him lead the people. God desires to place trustworthy men and women as Josephs, Daniels, and Esthers into the United Nations and various government organizations where they will effect change and do it with godly motives and conviction.

In some nations, world leaders, *kings,* may go to witches and warlocks for wisdom to make certain decisions but a godly marketplace leader can prophesy through word of knowledge or word of wisdom to unveil God's wisdom. An example of this is where the Lord had me prophesy to a senior-level manager *king* about changes that were going to take place in her department; and through the wisdom of God, I offered strategies on what changes she should make to be successful. This opened the door, where God created an environment of trust between us, where she asked for ongoing godly counsel. The prophetic is an access point that reveals God's heart in a situation or matter while providing divine instruction.

Current State of Affairs

Jesus said, "...you will hear of wars and threats of wars, but don't panic. Yes, these things must take place, but the end won't follow immediately. Nation will go to war against nation, and kingdom against kingdom. There will be earthquakes in many parts of the world, as well as famines" (Mark 13:7-8, NLT). M. K. Komi confirms this by saying all that is currently taking place throughout the nations, *"The Lord seems to be shaking every part of today's world. We are seeing financial upheaval, terrorism, wars, political tensions, moral decay, and unprecedented natural disasters."* As he points out that God is shaking His people to awaken them to their call, He's calling all Kingdom men and women to take their rightful positions of power and authority where they'll pray and prophesy over the nations of the world, so that His mercy and grace can cover the Earth.

As Kingdom influencers, we can speak peace over nations in war. We can command the storms to be still. As God is a God of righteousness, justice, and equality, we can decree that it is released in our cities, nations, regions, territories, and throughout the nations of the world.

Pursuit of Justice and Reformation

I am the daughter of parents that emigrated from Jamaica, West Indies to the U.S. in search of a better life. Growing up, my parents raised me in a household where we discussed many of the systemic issues that affected our community and society at large. I began developing a strong passion to help and advocate for those in need, especially after having personal experiences with social injustice. Years later, God opened the door for me to work in government for Hillary Rodham Clinton when she was at the time a New York State Senator. During this time, I gained exposure into some of the various statewide issues that affected constituents on a local level and learned how the government resolved these matters.

Soon after, the Lord moved me to the legal industry where He led me to strategically pray against different demonic agendas being pushed in New York City. Then, the Lord began to give me revelation about issues; not only on a local level, but also on a global level. This was followed by opening my eyes to see issues with social injustice affecting different ethnic and racial groups, gender inequality, and sexual exploitation of women and children in various parts of the world.

The Lord then began placing a strong burden on me for the nations, and instructed me to pray for doors to open for me in the United Nations where I could initiate change. He showed me that I would have more authority in prayer over nations because my presence there as a gatekeeper would affect the atmosphere and help to advance the Kingdom of God. As C. Peter Wagner said, *"The kingdom of God is within us, and we are the ones responsible for advancing it wherever we live and minister."* So, after fervently praying for close to a year, the Lord answered my prayers and supernaturally placed me in the organization. I currently work there, where I have been mandated by the Lord to strategically pray and intercede over local and international laws and policies, and various influential leaders and nations.

A Glance at the United Nations

The United Nations is an intergovernmental organization that allows world leaders to come together to discuss world affairs that affect their nations. They also provide global statistical data that allows nations to compare statistics with other nations. They can track the progress made over time in various categories that impact the growth or decline of a nation. It also allows us to examine changes in specific areas, such as violence against women, marriage, divorce statistics, etc. This provides a wonderful measuring stick because we can then strategically focus prayer in the areas where change is needed. Then we can refer back to the data to spiritually map the changes that occur over time. This will confirm if our prayers are hitting the mark or if we need to remain consistent in areas where a move of God is needed.

In *Apostolic Strategies Affecting Nations*, Dr. Jonathan David talks about how we can bring reformation to the society through prayer and various activities where the community will take notice. As we fervently pray against the powers of hell and target it towards the different issues that negatively impact nations, we'll begin to establish authority in the realm of the spirit that will cause breakthrough to take place. Dr. David states, *"When we touch the "spirit world" not only demons recognize and fear us; the community will sit up and take notice of our contribution to reforming the society."* Having the ecclesiastical backing in prayer will help us to overthrow demonic powers. This I believe will help us to cause social change and reformation where a major shift is needed throughout the nations of the world.

Governmental Decrees

1. I decree that all nations will seek and find Jesus Christ (Isaiah 65:1).
2. I decree that the fire of God will burn out all powers of hell, occultism, witchcraft, sorcery, and divination in all nations (Acts 19:19).
3. I decree that the fire of God is released and will destroy all idols throughout the nations of the world (Isaiah 2:18).

4. I decree that all apostolic and prophetic gatekeepers will emerge in all nations and take their rightful place (Lamentation 5:14).
5. I decree that the spirit of poverty, hunger and oppression is broken off the people of the nations of the world (Psalm 72:12-13).
6. I decree that sickness and disease are far from our bodies and people in all nations shall have excellent health (3 John 1:2).
7. I decree that righteousness, peace, and justice shall rule and reign in the nations of the world (Isaiah 32:1 & 7)
8. I decree that blessing of the Lord makes all nations and those that dwell therein rich and adds no sorrows to it (Proverb 10:22).
9. I decree that nation shall not lift up sword against nation, neither shall they learn war anymore (Isaiah 2:4).
10. I decree that God is placing God-fearing men and women in influential positions in the United Nations and throughout the governments of the world. And, every decision they make will be under the subjection of the Holy Spirit (Isaiah 60:3).

Prophetic Declarations

I prophesy to the nations of the world and decree peace (shalom) — an absence of war, hate, hostility, murder, wickedness, and evil. I decree all thrones of iniquity are dethroned throughout the nations and a release of judgment upon demonic kings. I prophesy that the blood of Jesus is released as a hedge of protection around the gates and borders of all nations where demonic forces cannot enter. I prophesy that the love of Christ is being shed abroad in all hearts. I prophesy healing and wealth throughout the nations. I prophesy that the nations of this world will begin to come together to resolve world issues in peace using godly wisdom. I prophesy that the spirit of justice, righteousness, and equality will rule and reign throughout the nations of the world in Jesus' Name.

---

[1] Marshall, R. (2000). *God@Work: Discovering the Anointing for Business.* Shippensburg, PA: Destiny Image Publishers, Inc., 1610.

[2] Komi, M.K. (2011). *The Prophetic Revelation of Haggai.* Shippensburg, PA: Destiny Image Publishers, Inc., 66.

[3] David, J. (1997). *Apostolic Strategies Affecting Nations* Johor, Malaysia: Rhema Images.

[4] Wagner, C. P. (2006). *The Church in the Workplace.* Ventura, CA: Regal Books,

KINGDOM STRATEGIES FOR THE MOUNTAIN OF GOVERNMENT

By Kenna O'Flannigan

The Word of God tells us in Romans 13:14 that there is no authority except from God, and the authorities that exist are appointed by God. The current condition of government has caused many to question the truth of this statement. There appears to be great division and contention amongst the leaders. This has caused people to feel unsafe. If we look to the Word to reveal a different perspective and context, this can assist in adjusting our vision away from current events and toward a larger picture to provide comfort, hope, and gain strategy to take the Mountain of Government.

If we look to the books of 1 & 2 Kings and 1 & 2 Chronicles, we can see a pattern for kings who, *"did evil in the sight of the Lord"* and the people they ruled followed their example (e.g. Ahab, Ahaziah, Jehoram, etc.). However, the Lord revealed to me that King Saul is a type of the current administration. King Saul was the first king following an extensive line of judges appointed by God through His prophets. Saul had no blueprint for the role of a king, as there had been no prior kings to draw from their experience. Similarly, the current White House administration does not have a background in law or politics. This characteristic was quite attractive to many voters in our nation. The people wanted someone "different," not a politician. In 1 Samuel, the cry for a "different" leader and advocate caused the Lord to allow King Saul to rule, and similarly, He has allowed Americans to choose the current leadership.

In some instances, the heart of the people can reflect the character of the leadership they choose. The current times reflect the character mentioned in 2 Timothy 3: *lovers of our own selves, covetous, boasters, proud, blasphemers, disobedient to parents, unthankful, unholy, without natural affection, trucebreakers, false accusers, incontinent, fierce, despisers of those that are good, traitors, heady, highminded, lovers of pleasures more than lovers of God; Having a form of godliness, but denying the power thereof.*

This crisis of character can be disheartening. However, as in all situations, the Scriptures offer us guidance and instruction on a strategy to respond.

First, we must be careful to examine ourselves within the Body of Christ for any of these characteristics before focusing on the condition outside of the Body. 1 Peter 4:17 clearly warns that judgment comes to God's House first. Knowing that the Lord protects His children, we must pray for mercy on the land; that wisdom and understanding enter the heart of the people and they change direction. Righteousness will exalt a nation, according to Proverbs 14:34.

An additional strategy to take the Mountain of Government is to have internal operatives—individuals established within the system to help effect change from the inside. There has been a long-standing argument whether the United States was founded as a Christian country. If we consider the religious background of the individuals in government, we can identify a pattern. According to Pew Research Center, nearly half of all presidents have been Christian (Episcopalian or Presbyterian)[1]. Currently, the 115th Congress of the United States is 91% Christian[2]. This percentage is higher than the national percentage of American adults that identify as Christian, which has decreased from 80% in 2008 to 75% currently[3]. If we take the time to review the constitution of all 50 states, God is mentioned in each preamble[4]. These numbers show evidence that believers are well-established in government and possess great opportunity to influence the law of the land.

As we can see from just these few statistics, the Lord has already installed internal operatives in government. Before sessions are started in the Congress, Senate, and House of Representatives, a prayer goes forth. This practice has long been a tradition in the United States government, as early as 1776 when the first chaplains were elected. The House of Representatives and Senate have chaplains elected to serve. Both local and national government open their meetings and sessions in prayer as a normal order of business. Strategic prayer by the internal operatives can serve to quickly dismantle any strongholds in government and can prevent the erection of idols and ungodly standards being established.

Therefore, we pray for the men and women whom God has established as internal operatives within government to gain greater revelation of strategy and wisdom to target their prayers and influence so that the Kingdom's influence becomes greater over the Mountain of Government. We pray that their influence over their colleagues and leadership cause them to turn their hearts to the Lord. We pray that these internal operatives walk in their integrity and be known for being men and women of godly character. May the Lord infuse them with boldness and courage to fight for righteousness and justice.

Another strategy to take this Mountain for the Lord is to be an external influence by voting. As believers, we must also be involved and knowledgeable in the day-to-day activities of politics. If we are not reading and learning what the various candidates stand for, if we are not running for office ourselves when we feel the leading of the Lord, if we are not voting in all elections, be it local government, congress, senate as well as the presidency, then it is the unbelievers who are deciding the people who run our country.

We must pray for the leaders. We must pray that godly people are elected to positions of authority and positions of influence. Prayer is essential, but it must be followed up with action. Voting is necessary to indicate that there is still a population of people that will support those in government. Such citizens are ready to support politicians who will take a stand for godly principles and legislation; fight for the oppressed and needy; and will not use their position to lord it over the people and become the oppressor. Voting and even becoming active in the political arena, if that is your purpose, will continue to show the nation and the world that there is still a remnant of people who will fight for the righteous result.

Prayerfully voting without regard to political party or personal agenda but with an eye toward God's purpose for government and protection of all people, can sway the direction of those in authority to recognize there is still a population of people interested in good and righteousness in the land.

Prayer Points and Declarations

1. The Lord is turning the heart of the king and all those in leadership away from wickedness and towards righteousness (Proverbs 21:1; Proverbs 16:12-13).
2. We pray that all of government operates in wisdom and understanding in all matters (Proverbs 12:1).
3. We pray that godly counsel surrounds our leaders and speak that multiple righteous counselors rise up, and leadership heeds godly counsel and walks with wise men (Proverbs 11:14; Proverbs 13:20; Proverbs 15:22; Proverbs 24:6).
4. We declare that the Lord is our Judge, the Lord is our Lawgiver, the Lord is our King; He will save us as we walk in obedience and righteousness to the authorities established by Him (Isaiah 33:22; Romans 13:14).
5. We seek you for discernment as we become more active in government process. We act in wisdom and godly counsel as we cast votes and choose who to support in every election; that this nation be exalted in righteousness (Proverbs 14:34).
6. Our hearts are humbled and broken. As we return to the Lord, He is building us up and sin is removed from our tents (Joel 2:13; Zechariah 1:3; Job 22:23; Lamentations 3:40).
7. As we repent and return to the Lord, He is returning to us (2 Chronicles 15:4).
8. We speak renewed fervor and passion for the Lord and seek revival throughout the land. We welcome the Holy Spirit as He ushers in healing and deliverance; that our latter is greater than our former (Hosea 6:1-3; Haggai 2:9).

We decree and declare that the will of the people is turned to righteousness and holiness. We declare that the hearts of those in the seat of the President, judges, lawmakers, and in all leadership, are in your hand, and we declare their hearts are turning back to you. We decree and declare that this nation is united in righteousness and holiness. We repent of past sins and idolatry and return to you. Please abide with us. We decree and declare that our nation is turning from our wicked ways before destruction comes. The scales are falling from our eyes to reveal wisdom and understanding of the truth, that we may come to the knowledge of the truth. We are chasing after you and your heart, and seek the riches of trusting in and following you. We declare that our hearts, minds, and intentions have turned back to you, Lord, as you lead us in righteousness. We decree that righteousness shall exalt this nation. Amen.

---

[1] Pew Research Center, http://www.pewresearch.org/fact-tank/2017/01/20/almost-all-presidents-have-been-christians/

[2] http://www.pewforum.org/2017/01/03/faith-on-the-hill-115/

[3] http://news.gallup.com/poll/187955/percentage-christians-drifting-down-high.aspx

[4] http://www.bebaptized.org/u.htm

THE WILLIE LYNCH CURSE: A Spiritual Battle We Must Win!

By Jackie Betty

Racism: An Established Evil

As I contemplated writing on this serious issue of institutional racism and inequality, a vision I had, over a year ago, came center-stage in my mind. It happened at an all-night prayer meeting. As I prayed against racism, I saw an old letter. I knew this document was very old because the paper was aged, yellowish-brown in color. The corners of the letter were burnt. As we continued to pray, we sensed that the vision revealed the Willie Lynch Letter.

As I researched, the Holy Spirit revealed other elements of this letter. Thompson and Beale indicate that dreams or visions with elements of burning can signify torment, being consumed by something, as well as having to deal with past issues.

Torment fits the landscape of the letter in this vision. Slaves were severely and inhumanely tortured.

Burnt also speaks of betrayal, one being let down by another or being sacrificed. At the time of the vision, I felt something ominous, even darkness and a vacuum in my spirit. We know all too well the decay and torture that slaves in America endured up to the nineteenth century. Willie Lynch, in his 1712 letter, referring to slaves as "valuable stock" said, "I caught the whiff of a dead slave hanging from a tree a couple of miles back" (p. 6). These words may be extremely hard for some readers to digest as they were for me, but thank God, our hope is not in loss or despair due to our suffering, but we trust in Jehovah *Gibbor*, our mighty warrior. We will not only heal, but we will win as well.

For many months, I kept revisiting the elements of this vision. I kept asking the Holy Spirit to tell me why He gave it to me. Months later, I purchased a copy of the book, "The Willie Lynch Letter & Making of a Slave." As I began to read, my stomach started to churn. The contents of this letter are awfully gruesome. I had to lean heavily on the Holy Spirit for sustenance and grace. Moreover, from the onset of this 28-page document, I sensed in my spirit that the enemy of our souls went straight for our minds. "…break them from one form of mental life to another… Keep the body and take the mind" (Lynch, p. 13).

As I contemplated, the Holy Spirit said to me, "I want you to write a book of decrees and declarations to counter the curses in this letter." Hence, this chapter, empowered by the Holy Spirit, forcefully establishes decrees and declarations that will dismantle all mind-controlling spirits that sit on these mountains of influence.

These decrees speak strongly to every high thing that has sought to distort our minds. Slaves were broken not only by horrendous physical acts but also by devious words that were carefully plotted to destroy a people whom God created in His image. It seems that these words had the capacity to inflict deadly mutilating blows that have crippled people for centuries. Lynch said, "Distrust is stronger than trust" (p. 8). We know that is a lie spoken by Satan, the father of lies. Suspicion, doubt, and unbelief are what the enemy of our souls desires.

We reject and denounce these lies from our consciousness. They do not determine our destiny as a people. Jesus clearly tells us that He is the Truth. He invites us in Proverbs to trust in Him with all our hearts and not to lean on our own understanding. Our trust is clear. Our trust is hope, faith, confidence, and conviction in Christ's power. The power of His Word overthrows all ill-spoken words and curses ever spoken over our race. While Satan used Lynch to plant "fear, distrust, and envy for control purposes," we use the living Word of God to destroy all fear, distrust, and envy. We have the mind of Christ. No weapons through a letter will conquer His purposes.

As I read and prayed, I started seeing the Holy Spirit as my Counselor. It is from this perspective of His person that I present Him to you. Here, I concentrate on Him as *Paraclete,* the Counselor. Bringing this side of the Holy Spirit closer home to our mental capacity, I call Him our Spiritual Psychologist. One definition of psychology is the science of the mind or of mental states and processes. The psychologist is a specialist in psychology. The Holy Spirit is the Psychologist. John 14:26 speaks of Him as Counselor who will remind us of all things. He gives us renewed minds. He tells us that our minds can be miraculously transformed with our spoken words.

"Neuroscientists have discovered that repetitive thoughts form neutral pathways as neurons. As these neurons fire together, they get wired together. Thus, the more a thought or belief is repeated and reinforced, the stronger these neural pathways become and the more automatically they become our way of thinking" (Sara Bernard). Wow! Discovery? Not really. The Holy Spirit, the greatest neuroscientist already revealed in Job's time that through divine relationship with the Father, Job could decree a thing and it shall be established (Job 22:28). These words, breathed with faith, become alive, sharper than a two-edged sword. Therefore, as we purposefully give voice to these decrees and declarations repeatedly, the Holy Spirit will reprogram our thinking. He will renew our minds. He will spiritually delete all forms of evil and wicked programming purposed in this letter written over 300 years ago. We will destroy this spirit of evil indoctrination from all mountains: Mountain of Culture, Arts and Entertainment, Media, Business, Education, Religion, Government, and yes, Family.

Through our decrees and declarations, we will burn these spirits that sear our minds: spirits of darkness, murder, evil, racism, and rage. These spirits will no longer stifle or kill our dreams. Our Father has said, "I know the plans I have for you, to prosper you and give you an expected end." It's time to connect to the Holy Spirit, the Psychotherapist, the true Psychologist. He is our Counselor. "The Counselor, the Holy Spirit, whom the Father will send in My name, he will teach you all things, and will remind you of all that I said to you" (John 14:26 WEB). Now, He says, you are a people of greatness. I have transformed you: mind, will, and intellect. Declare it to the mountains!

Holy Spirit Mind Power Builder

- The Lord our God sets us high above all nations of the Earth (Deuteronomy 28).
- Therefore, my mind is blessed and overtaken with fruitful, peaceful, and creative things: strength, ideas, and inventions. Surely, the Lord blesses all the works of my hand—they stem from my renewed mind.
- He makes me head and never tail; therefore, I am not inferior in any way in my mind or in my thoughts.
- I know my God, and I do exploits for His glory (Daniel 11: 32).
- I am who God says I am: fearfully and wonderfully made (Psalm 139: 1).

Holy Spirit Pain Eradicator

- Old things are passed away. Look, all things are new in Christ (2 Corinthians 5:17).
- I forget the former things, for Christ gives me new, prosperous thoughts.
- I reject and eradicate all painful memory of slavery and its torture.
- I eradicate all mind-tangling pain due to injustice, hatred, and racism.
- The surging power of Christ's blood purges my memory of all acts of slavery.
- My past of torture and abuse has died.
- My mind is radically renewed in Christ.
- I feed my mind on lovely, pure, and just things (Philippians 4:8).
- Death and life reside in my tongue, so I speak life to my future (Proverbs 18:21).
- I speak death to the curses in Willie Lynch's letter.
- I have whatever I say: I say my mind is empowered with greatness in Christ (Mark 11:24)

Holy Spirit Mind Rejuvenator

- For the Word of God is alive and active. Sharper than any double-edged sword, it penetrates even to dividing soul and spirit, joints and marrow; it judges the thoughts and attitudes of the heart (Hebrews 4: 12 NIV).
- I am renewed in the spirit of my mind (Ephesians 4:23).
- Abba's love floods my heart, mind, and soul (Matt. 22: 37).
- I have the mind of Christ (I Corinthians 2:16).
- Therefore, my mind has plan, purpose, and perspective.
- The wisdom I have is not of this world. It is God's perfect wisdom.
- My mind is retrained by the Holy Spirit; it will not conform to the pattern of this world (Romans 2:12).
- We will not conform to any reversing of roles as Black males and females.
- Our minds understand and accept who God created us to be.
- Our men are the head of our household.
- Our females are the nurturers.
- No force of darkness can twist our minds.

We are a people of greatness; a peculiar, royal priesthood; and a generation chosen to walk in Christ's marvelous light (1 Peter 2: 9).

As we decree and declare, we build boulders of spiritual power. Through the Holy Spirit, we move mountains. Hallelujah!

Note to Reader:

The author is aware of some controversy pertaining to the validity of the letter of 1712. However, historically-documented evidence supports the horrific murderous acts of slavery: raping, torturing, maiming, and even burning of Blacks in that time.

[1] Bernard, Sara. "Neuroplasticity: Learning Physically Changes the Brain." *Edutopia*, 1 Dec. 2010, www.edutopia.org/neuroscience-brain-based-learning-neuroplasticity.

[2] Lynch, William. "The Willie Lynch Letter and the Making of a Slave." *The Willie Lynch Letter and the Making of a Slave*, African Tree Press, 2017, pp. 6–8.

[3] Thompson, Adam F., and Adrian Beale. *The Divinity Code to Understanding Your Dreams and Visions*. Destiny Image, 2011.

CHAPTER 8

A 7 MOUNTAIN FORECAST: WHERE DO WE GO FROM HERE?

By Dr. Yolanda Powell

The Evangelical Baton & the Apostolic-Prophetic Movement

In August of 1975, evangelical leaders Bill Bright, founder of Campus Crusade, and Loren Cunningham, founder of Youth with a Mission, had lunch together in Colorado. God simultaneously had given these two men a mighty message in prayer that would ultimately impact how the world could be effectively evangelized for Christ Jesus. During that same time frame, Francis Schaeffer, leader of the L'Abri Community in Switzerland received the same divine directive. The message they were given was revolutionary. It redirected Believers to impact societies and transform nations by bringing a stronger influence and expert presence to the seven spheres or mountains of culture that constitute the pillars of society.

Eventually, these seven mountains were identified as religion, family, education, government, business/finance, media/communications, and arts and entertainment. In essence, the Holy Spirit was helping these evangelical change-agents to know where the battlefield was really arrayed. It was inside culture—where humanity is constantly bombarded and impacted in every way. Culture was the strategic territory of focus, not foreign mission as many supposed. The hearts and minds of people were encased in the cultural framework of life, and souls would be won or lost based on that knowledge. Their assignment was to raise up like-minded thought-leaders to scale the mountains and aggressively train a new generation of *movers and shakers* to understand the larger narrative of Kingdom Advancement as outlined in Matthew 6:10, *"Thy Kingdom come, thy will be done on Earth as it is in Heaven."*

Clearly, these seven mountains will either be influenced by the righteous and our Christ-led principles, or by the wiles and lies of the devil's kingdom. We must play big and climb high to not only influence the people on these mountains, but to expose and depose the principalities and demonic princes that rule as ancient fiefdoms at their peaks.

Depose Demons & Unseat Principalities: Our Kingdom Mandate

It was on this latter point —about wickedness, powers, and darkness, that the Lord began to reveal to me in the spring of 2015. I had been called several years earlier to expand my Kingdom work and become a Marketplace Apostle. So, I invested in coaches and *train the trainer* programs to expand my skill-set and business acumen; as I transitioned from the comforts of ministry to the thoroughfare of culture.

Later that year I was privileged to minister on the platform of Apostle John Eckhardt's Impact Conference. In preparation for that event, the Lord spoke prophetically about the 7 Mountains and instructed me to tell Eckhardt and my spiritual father, Apostle Axel Sippach, what the Lord was instructing. His words were sharp and piercing, "I am taking the baton from the Evangelicals," the Lord said emphatically. "And I'm putting it in the hands of the Apostolic-Prophetic Movement, for it is your time to dispossess the principalities that rule these mountains." It was a profound word with far-reaching ramifications. But I was obedient.

Several months later, Apostle Axel responded to the prophetic and launched out into the deep to begin a radical Jesus Movement called EPIC (Extraordinary People Influencing Culture). He heard God and the next phase of the 7 Mountain Mandate was born in the loins of apostles and prophets. The irony is that it had been 40 years (a complete generation) almost to the day, when EPIC was born in August 2015. The baton was thrust into our hands and we were pressed to run hard and run high to *deal with the demons* who plagued and prostituted those mountains as an unseen, impenetrable force. Where the Evangelical (during Phase I) were required to train, appoint, and release disciples; we were being called to raise, activate, and release warriors on the mountains to deal with the devil, even as we served the people.

The Apostolic-Prophetic Movement is a strategic, tactical weapon in the hand of the Lord to fulfill Genesis1:26, "And God said, Let us make man in our image, after our likeness: and let them have dominion over the fish of the sea and over the fowl of the air, and over the cattle, and over all the earth, and over every creeping thing that creeps upon the earth."

We are seriously committed to this biblical mandate, as those trained and exercised in Kingdom areas of apostolic pioneering, prophetic intercession, disruptive innovation, miracle deliverance, and wealth generation in order to effectively executive Satan's defeat and reclaim territory for our King. Despite evangelistic discipleship making for almost four decades, the ruling powers on the 7 Mountains would never take down and desist their evil maneuvers without a frontal attack and offensive fight. So, apostles and prophets along with apostolic and prophetic Believers have been given a grace to penetrate and prevail with covert plans of attack that are Heaven-sent and angel-enforced to depose demons and unseat principalities. It's an exciting time to be alive and to partner with the Lord in these stratagems.

As a result of what the Lord has spoken and unveiled, the Apostolic-Prophetic Movement has already begun to make an impact on the 7 Mountains that will span far into the future. There is no more powerful strategy for taking full control of the seven mountains than by **conquering and ruling** through these seven (7) areas of mastery:

1. Apostolic pioneering
2. Prophetic intercession
3. Miracle deliverance
4. Vocal invasion/story liberation
5. Creative solutions/problem solving

6. Disruptive innovation/business design
7. Wealth generation

Almighty God has equipped His apostolic and prophetic offspring as a *secret weapon* that will cause the mountains to shake and tremble, as we annihilate and conquer these illegal, demonic occupants and restore order, social justice, and financial equity to the nations; while rebranding Christ in culture and establishing mercy and righteousness to all. These miraculous victories will be seen in the near future, and they will far exceed what was done in the last 100 years or even by the early Church. It's an exciting time to be alive in the Kingdom.

Forecast #1
Apostolic Pioneering: Hubs of Synergy & Connectivity

As we encounter the enemies upon each of the seven mountains, we must keep our spiritual ears tuned into Heaven's channel and dialed into the needs of culture. In the future, seasoned apostles will pioneer social systems with great skill and an enormous capacity to outline community hubs of interface where the Church and state collaborate; corporations and marketplace ministers create products and services; and nations negotiate with diplomacy and global peace beyond what the world has known heretofore. *"The wolf and the lamb shall graze together, and the lion shall eat straw like the ox; and dusts shall be the serpent's food. They shall do no evil or harm in all My holy mountain," says the Lord"* (Isaiah 65:25).

Apostles will use their governing gifts and metrons of wisdom to heal, restore, and create communities and regions in way that will astound the global village. Social reform will be birthed through their loins, and a new awakening of connectivity and unity will be released throughout the seven continents. An anointing for synergy and unity will flow upon the seven mountains and the wolf nature in mankind will be subject to the nature of the lamb. The lion mentality of domination will adhere to the simplicity of the ox. The striking destruction of serpent personalities shall be changed internally and humbled to go low. Evil will meet its match and good shall consume it. The Lord's will and desires will fill the Earth and restoration will cover it.

Forecast #2

Prophetic Intercession: Prophets & Warriors Arise & Slay!

An advance battalion of prophets and a vast brigade of prophetic warriors will be positioned and/or hired by companies, colleges, churches, and civic groups in varied places throughout the mountains to wage strategic intercessions and warfare in varied areas from crime and gang violence to low test scores and employment statistics.

Those called and gifted to pray and intercede will serve a vital role throughout the nations with measurable change being calculated in the realms. With great results and outcomes, the Kingdom will advance and darkness will no longer sustain blinders over the hearts of men.

In every nation and culture, the Lord searches to promote those who stand upon the mountains of society to intercede for those complex and intricate issue-sloped terrains. Each of us has a proclivity to pray for a certain mountain because of the way God made us. But there are those who are skillfully wired to strategize and war in a way that will outwit, outthink, and outsmart the devil. More and more, we will see these intercessors emerge and slay the adversarial forces. And as Isaiah prophesied, "Everyone there will stare at you and ask, 'Can this be the one who shook the Earth and made the kingdoms (mountains) of the world tremble!" Arise Prophets, Slay Warriors! This is your greatest hour.

Forecast #3

Miracle Healing & Deliverance: Personal Conflict, Social Disorder, Mental Illness Cast Out!

With an understanding of global dominion and our assent to take the tops of the seven mountains, Romans 8:18-27 suddenly 'comes alive like never before,' unveiling that if God's physical creation suffers from corruption, then surely the seven mountains of culture also suffer under this same bondage. The *groanings* we hear in life and culture are directly due to torments and sufferings by strongholds and demonic systems.

Without doubt, each of the seven mountains of influence has its own effects upon the inhabitants of the Earth. And whomever sits atop those mountains have control over the society and its culture. While ancient principalities rule and spew conflict, disorder, and illness, mankind can never be pain free. Therefore, the miracle of deliverance will be highly sought out and called upon in areas of personal devastation, social disorder, and mental chaos.

Kingdom believers who are astute in this area of ministry will be greatly used in the lives of individuals, communities, and institutions where miracles can flourish and the captive be set free! This will defy the norm and status quo and much healing and joy will fill the landscape.

The Mission of Christ will be carried out in both ministry and marketplace as revealed in Luke 4:18-19, *"The Spirit of the Lord is upon Me, because He has anointed Me to preach the gospel to the poor; He has sent me to heal the brokenhearted, to proclaim liberty to the captives and recovery of sight to the blind, to set at liberty those who are oppressed, to proclaim the acceptable year of the Lord."* As we handle the affairs of our King on the Mountains, we will remove the hindrances that have sustained these systemic ills in society. Miracles will be seen in the public square and healing and deliverance will become a staple that unveils the Father's love and care for His children.

Forecast #4
Vocal Invasion: The Liberation of Beautiful Feet on the Mountains

> *"How then, can they call on the ne they have not believed in? And how can they believe in the one of whom they have not heard? And how can they hear without a preacher? And how can they preach unless they are sent? As it is written, "How beautiful [on the mountains] are the feet of those who bring good news." Romans 10:14-15*

This scripture verse literally transformed my life, ministry, and business a few years ago. I was doing a word study in Greek on "preacher" and "beautiful." Understanding their meaning brought revelation and an apostolic strategy for what I call 'Vocal Invasion'. There is tremendous power in the human voice to tell of the "good things" that the Lord alone has done in one's life. But, where there is trauma or deep pain, the voice is often muted and the ability to communicate and articulate your story is silenced.

The prophets of old and the Apostle Paul all refer to "beautiful feet" moving swiftly across the mountains. There is coming restoration and healing to the vocal chords of the Believers who have been shut down by horrific issues of life pain, family wounds, and Church hurt. Many were targeted by Satan as young children through abuse, molestation, rape, rejection, abandonment, abortion, divorce, drugs, poverty, and every other kind of pain point. They have lived through the terror, yet because of their faith in Jesus Christ, they have recovered lost treasure and regained their vocal power. These are the ones that will invade the seven mountains in the years ahead. They are not preachers per se, but public speakers, proclaiming and heralding the "good news" of their personal story. They have been liberated and set free and have a voice to speak to the issues with conviction, persuasion, and liberation.

The word **beautiful** (Strong's #5611/ oraioi / ho-rah-yos) means "belonging to the right season or hour. To flourish and be at full bloom or development." The word **preacher** (Strong's #2784 / kerusso' / kay-roos'-so) is simply to proclaim, herald, to speak persuasively and with conviction, to speak in public. So, what I foresee on the seven mountains is an army of 'power speakers' invading the public square, telling their story in such a way that others are drawn to the Way, Truth & Light and the liberation He offers to all despite race, gender, social status, or nationality. This is revolutionary in the marketplace and will motivate the masses.

Forecast #5

Creative Problem Solving: Genuinely Serving, Giving & Caring

The world is looking for solutions to complex problems in society. Therefore, Kingdom Believers must be about solving problems. The true Christos message brings liberty to the captives, not through control or manipulation, but through a self-sacrificing, non-judgmental love that the world has never seen or experienced before.

This is highlighted in the story of the Samaritan woman. Jesus talked with her. The disciples were quietly irritated that Jesus talked to her. Samaritans were off limits culturally (not the right political party, or the right skin color). She was also a woman. That alone was reason to avoid her altogether. But, Jesus is a rule breaker. He speaks. He touches. He builds relationships—across all restrictions. As a result, she was deeply impacted by His words; and went into the city as a "public herald" and "power speaker" to share (i.e. preach) her experience to her family and friends. He had addressed a concern and answered a question in her soul, which ultimately changed her life. Those in the city came to see Jesus and He spent several days there as a result. The Kingdom was expanded in that region by two pivotal areas: story and solution. *"And many of the Samaritans of that city believed in Him because of the word of the woman who testified, "He told me all that I ever did."*

Creative problem-solving, when administered with genuine serving, giving, and caring can reform society. When we operate from love and service, we will be attractive to the world. They will desire to follow. We become solution-providers to the issues of mankind. Jesus solved people's problems, which resulted in a greater influence in people's lives.

Jesus modeled influence while he was on Earth by building relationships and solving people's problems by serving them. Jesus said that if you want to be great, you must be servant of all. *For even the Son of Man did not come to be served, but to serve, and to give His life a ransom for many"* (Mark 10:45).

Forecast #6
Disruptive Innovation: Designing Businesses That Promote People, Planet & Profits

As a result of our successful dominion on the seven mountains and the overthrow of principalities, Kingdom Believers will liberally design and implement *cutting edge* businesses, non-profit organizations, training centers, and trade schools in a way that produces disruptive innovation in a free market economy.

The approach to the bottom line will consider the outcome for people and its effect on the planet, alongside the amount of profit to be made. This will bring disruption to greed and corruption, as greater populations choose witty inventions and wise innovations that bring life, sustain a healthy Earth and build financial wealth for succeeding generations.

Kingdom Believers will be able to canvas the field of life and creative *out of the box* ideas, products, and services that will alter, increase, and expand consumers; while transforming capitalism as it has existed void of a Christ-like core and center.

Just the way ordinary businesses create a Unique Positioning in the marketplace, (think WaWa over 7-11 or Chick-fil-A over KFC), I foresee unprecedented business models arising on the mountains that will be forged through vision, dreams, and prophetic utterance. A supernatural energy and vitality will flow from its mission, recalibrating how small and large companies operate and function. So, "be diligent in business," for something spectacular is being produced within the Body of Jesus Christ in this hour for a future time. *"Do you see any truly competent workers? They will serve kings rather than working for ordinary people"* (Proverbs 22:29).

Forecast #7
Wealth Generation: The Power to Command Currency & Economy

The Scriptures declare, "but you shall remember the Lord your God, for it is He who is giving you power to make wealth, that He may confirm His covenant which He swore to your fathers as it is this day" Deuteronomy 8:18. As Kingdom Believers access increasing freedom to greater levels in every area of life: spirit, soul, and body–a fresh capacity to gain, create, and acquire wealth will begin to evolve and manifest. Our containers, cupboards, and coffers will overflow with new wine and much grain–we will utilize our God-given gifts and talents to multiply and compound what we already possess.

Over time, a new wisdom for currency exchange, economic expansion, and financial flourishing will overtake those who have been diligent to invest wisely in their own ideas. A new bastion of millionaires will emerge from obscure places and rise to the top of Forbes. Unknown gatekeepers will ascend and arise from the presence of God with a heart to manage seven-figure portfolios.

It's going to be an astounding epoch of time, when Joseph rules Egypt, Daniel leads Babylon, and Esther reigns in Persia once again. Many of you are exiting your seasons of hardship, rejection, and murder – to take the heads of companies, run for political offices, sit in counsel with nobles, and even teach the kings of the Earth. The forecast is sure, that as we take the Mountains…religion will be decimated, families restored, education strengthened, government revitalized, business maximized, media deregulated, and arts and entertainment purified. What a glorious season is before us. Arise and let us take the top. The seven mountains are in need of us as the heirs of salvation and the true sons of God!

MEET THE CO-AUTHORS

Tony & Nicole Davis

Tony and Nicole Davis reside in Owings Mills, Maryland. They have been married over 25 years, and have the honor of parenting two adult sons. As co-authors and family and marriage mentors, they have purposed to create thought-provoking, soul-searching, behavior-altering devotionals for couples, parents, and individuals to read over and over. Their aim is to be catalysts in showing people how to establish their desired relationship experiences—at home or in the marketplace. They are also co-founders of Empower to Engage, a Christian based organization designed to equip men and women with resources and strategies to become effective leaders. Tony and Nicole believe people must first be able to lead themselves well and then exemplify this leadership in every area of their lives: thus, empowering them to impact our evolving society for good. For more resources offered by Tony and Nicole, visit
www.empowertoengage.com

Sarafia Jones-Hall

Evangelist Sarafia Jones-Hall is a native of Waco TX. and has been commissioned to the great city of Houston TX. She is married to Prophet Samuel Hall. They have 2 sons and daughter-in-law. Evangelist Hall has been charged to preach the word in the prison, as well as abuse shelters and community. Evangelist Hall operates under a strong prophetic- teaching anointing in dance, prayer, intercession; . Her calling and passion are to impart deliverance, healing, and true worship to the lost and unlearned through equipping and importation, releasing the fire to stir up their gifts.

Through much abuse, rejection, and being left for dead, Evangelist Hall dropped out of junior high school feeling great desperation. In spite of her situation she was given a way of escape, her love for dance. Her first sermon came through prophetic dance. Through dance ministry, it pushed out her first Book. "Spirit and Flesh Dancing Together As One" Evangelist Hall wrote her 2nd Book, My Chapter 2016 Journey. Evangelist Sarafia Hall Graduated from ELST Ministry and Mentoring School in 2017. To learn more about her ministry and books. Go to sarafiahallbooks.com or email her at sarafiahallmin@gmail.com

Donita Gordon

Rev. Donita Gordon was born and raised in Norfolk, VA, USA. Her commitment to lifelong learning has pushed her to obtain a Bachelor's of Science (B.S.) from Norfolk State University, Masters of Education (M.Ed.) from Cambridge College, Educational Specialist Degree (Ed.S.), and a candidate for Doctor of Strategic Leadership (DSL) from Regent University. Rev. Gordon is married to Nicholas Gordon and together they have 3 children. She is the Care Pastor of Immanuel Worship Deliverance Ministries, Intl. in Norfolk, VA, USA where she is ordained in the Gospel. She serves under the leadership of Rev. Dr. Virginia Barnett, senior pastor. After fifteen years of experience in the public education sector, Rev. Donita Gordon was able to pursue a passionate career working with incarcerated juveniles. Her ministerial gifts and love for teaching prompted her to start Curating the Arts parachurch ministry. Since 2010, she has worked to cultivate the youth in the areas of visual and performing arts. Rev. Gordon has a passion for International Missions and Evangelism. The Doctor of Strategic Leadership degree helped to foster a ministry to offer global consulting and strategic leadership in the areas of Prophetic Worship (arts, dance), Global Evangelism (jail, missions, street evangelism) , and Soaking prayers (Prayer Manual). Her ministry has served in the USA, China, Jamaica, London, and Ghana helping to carry out the Great Commission and fulfill the mandate to serve and save souls.

Michelle Brown

Michelle "Michl" Brown is an ordained Apostolic-Deliverance Prophet who is well known for her strong zeal, genuine love for people and desire to see them healed, delivered and living a victorious life of fulfilled prophetic destiny. She serves a dual role in the Kingdom of God by also impacting the nations as a Marketplace Minister at the United Nations where she witnesses the love and power of Christ.

As God's Prophet, she has been mandated with ensuring that justice prevails, saints are empowered, set free from bondage and God's design for creation manifests that causes a global transformation throughout the nations. Prophetess McKoy is a lover of Jesus, advocate for justice, social reformer, entrepreneur and empowerment coach. With her strong love for Christ and dedication to Kingdom advancement, she thrives on training and equipping believers so they can advance in their prophetic destinies. Her mandate is to impact individuals, the Mountain of Government & Business and the nations so that they can come into divine alignment with God's original plans and purposes for the Earth.

Prophetess McKoy is the visionary and founder of Prophetic Charge Ministries in Bronx, NY and a member of E.P.I.C. Network under the leadership of Apostle Axel Sippach.

Cherie Banks

Cherie Banks is the mastermind behind the moniker, CEO Influencer™. Her visionary leadership contributed to generating the 1st billion dollars for an international Fortune 500 company with consecutive results. She is a success leader, business investor, and serial entrepreneur with a multi-million dollar brand. Cherie is a highly-sought after industry expert for her business mastery, strategic planning, market penetration, growth expansion, global alliance, leadership development, ethical integrity, PR/media relations, crisis management, conflict resolution, and human capital commitment. She also serves as a chief strategic advisor, fiduciary board member, and social good advocate for non-profit organizations. Cherie is an honored recipient of prestigious awards in business, law, education, and community.

Notably, Cherie is an apostolic visionary and prophetic voice in marketplace ministry with a profound anointing in business, wealth, and legacy. She serves as a pastoral confidant and spiritual advisor to CEOs, corporations, church leaders, and faith-based ministries. Cherie has an M.A. in Pastoral Studies from Loyola University and an Honorary Doctorate in Divinity. She also has a J.D. from Loyola University School of Law and a B.A. from DePaul University. Cherie was a founding board member and vice magistrate of Phi Delta Phi Honorary Legal Fraternity. She studied European law at Oxford University in the United Kingdom. Additionally, Cherie was distinguished as a United States honorary guest at the European Parliament, Council of Europe, European Courts of Justice and Human Rights, European Union, and NATO. Cherie earned highest honors distinction for academic excellence and moral character with notoriety on the President's Scholar Guild, Golden Key International Honor Society, and National Dean's List.

Alexander Gray

Apostle Dr. Alexander Gray's ministry began with a divine visitation from the LORD in 1992 when the LORD delivered him from crack cocaine addiction, alcoholism and homelessness. Apostle Gray flows powerfully in the Healing Ministry as well as the Prophetic. He is the founder and Pastor of Living Love Ministries International, Inc. of Bronx, New York. Apostle Gray is a motivational speaker, a NYC Chaplain under the NY Chaplain of Community Affairs Bureau and a published author. His first book "Nuggets of Revelation from on High" was released in April 2014. He is in the process of releasing his second book, "Send Judah into the Battle". Apostle Gray has had the opportunity to preach throughout the United States as well as internationally. He is also the founder of "Wings of Faith International Outreach" a community based organization that speaks to his heart's cry which is to help the youth. Apostle Dr. Alexander Gray's vision is to produce the proof that Jesus is alive.

Email: apostle44@gmail.com
www.apostlealexandergray7.com
Phone: 646 209 5473
P.O. Box 670024
Bronx, NY 10467

Jonelle Maxwell

Apostle Jonelle Maxwell is a traveling Apostolic Reformer commissioned to the nations, primarily the 7 Mountains. God uses Apostle Jonelle as a conduit to be a sign and a wonder in the earth. Apostle Jonelle is a voice of the dejected, displaying the justice of God. Because of her passion to set the captives free, she will go to the deepest extreme being led by the Holy Spirit. Apostle Jonelle Maxwell is definitely one that walks in the Isaiah 58 mandate. She is a repairer of the wasted places.

Thapelo Kgabage

Thapelo Donald Kgabage was born in a town called Taung, Leshobo Village (Mokgareng) located in the North West province, South Africa and currently residing at Potchefstroom (North West Province, South Africa). Thapelo is a certified accountant by profession and works as an auditor for the South African Supreme Audit Institution. He is also a business-man running a consultation company that has helped many companies with its administrations and major projects.

Thapelo is a young ordained minister of the Gospel of Jesus Christ who began preaching the Gospel of the Lord Jesus Christ at a very young age of 10 years. He is a conference speaker, motivational speaker, mentor, the author of the book entitled "The Benjamin Generation" and he has been involved in lot of ministries including outreaches as well as crusades across South Africa. Thapelo has impacted many lives around the communities he is based, and he is much known for the sound prophetic and apostolic teachings, he also worked and helped establish many ministries with the teachings and the administration ability.

Joy A. Witter

Joy A. Witter is a Prophetic voice to the Nations. She is a teacher with a Bachelor Degree in education. She is a gifted teacher, persuasive writer, speaker and visionary. She has a mandate to be a light to the Nations with a demonstration of the supernatural power of God. She is passionate and driven to impact and influence nations. She is co-author in the "Speak to the mountain" Anthology, speaking to the Education Mountain.

Carla Wallace

Carla Wallace is the business owner of M.O.Y.A. Productions, LLC and Centurion Health and Wellness Solutions, LLC. She is a Registered Nurse, who is currently employed by a national health care company in the Market Place as a Regional Nurse Consultant for the Texas region. She is an author, a mentor and a sponsor to many Kingdom Business Owners and start- up companies. She is a visionary who carries the Joseph anointing, who loves equipping, empowering and launching people into the things that will help advance the Kingdom of God. She is an Ambassador with a Kingdom Business with marketplace influence.

Alandis Porter

Apostle Alandis is a seasoned Apostolic voice and prophetic teacher with a down to earth style. She carries a heavy healing and deliverance mantle. She is an Apostle of love, intercession and wealth. Committed to building and educating others to exemplify the heart of God.

Apostle Alandis is currently the visionary of Kingdom Advancement Global Ministries, the Dean and an instructor in the T.E.A.R.S Training Academy, the Apostolic covering and overseer of Kingdom Advancers Global Network, Radio Personality and published author.

Tressena Jones

Tressena's passion is to see young people successfully navigate life into adulthood because they have learned the importance of making the right choices and will maximize every opportunity their education gives. The alignment of her vocation and her calling has brought purpose and direction to her ministry outside of the four walls of the church.

As an Educator, she is concerned with the present state of public education. She has used her voice to speak at public education rallies, for the support and safety of students at school board meetings and to encourage politicians to also become advocates and supporters of public education through funding. As an advocate, she supports students and teachers because she believes education is the great equalizer and is a very important work.

Amanda Samuels

Amanda Samuels is an Author, Speaker, and Entrepreneur. She brings a broad background of leadership, business, coaching, training, management and marketing skills, and expertise to help clients grow their business. As a servant leader, she is passionate about equipping and empowering believers to fulfill purpose. Amanda currently resides in Guyana, South America and enjoys reading, writing, nature viewing, and traveling. To contact author, please send an email to amanda20_samuels@yahoo.com.

LaDonna Jackson

Prefacing her salvation at the age of 20, LaDonna Jackson had a generational "birthright" to a call in ministry. Her family moved from Kansas City, Kansas to Houston, Texas when she was very young. Soon after, LaDonna became adamant about her marketplace pursuits. She obtained three college degrees: BA (Sociology/Human Development and Family Studies); BM (Music Education); and MM (Voice Performance). In the near future, she plans to pursue an MA and PhD in speech language and pathology to become a fully licensed singing voice specialist. Her desire is to study voice disorders and become a voice coach for many, including those in Hollywood. Other than marks in education, LaDonna has had an opera singing career onstage with appearances in Carnegie Hall, Uganda, and the Amalfi Coast. Her next step is to turn these opportunities into global missions.

LaDonna currently serves at Free Indeed Church International in Houston, Texas, under the leadership of Apostle Johnny and Prophetess Jenice Gentry. She is actively involved in the prison ministry aspect of Community Works CDC, a non profit geared towards missions, and the re-entry of ex-offenders into society. She is also involved in Free Squad, the ministry's evangelism team.

Shelby Frederick

Shelby Frederick, who is affectionately known by her social media followers as "Lady Jewels", is a rising apostolic prophetic leader whose unique communication style bridges generational gaps, using "Life Keys" to convey kingdom principles for successful living. She is the founder of God's Precious Jewels, a women's ministry which has birthed several extensions including Jewels Speak Radio Show, War Room Warriors Prayer Ministry and Sisterhood Fellowship.

With over a decade of experience as a Licensed Massage Therapist, her knowledge and training allows her to holistically educate the public on the benefits of alternative therapies, including the incorporation of essential oils in daily living. Her vision as a Wellness Specialist is to equip women with holistic strategies, inspiring them to take personal responsibility for their emotional wellness as they make positive impacts in their spheres of influence.

Kenna O'Flannigan

Kenna O'Flannigan accepted Jesus as her Savior and Lord in 1994. Four years later, she received and embraced the Lord's call to ministry. As an office gift to the Body of Christ, Kenna operates as a watchman prophet inspired by Holy Spirit.

Elder Kenna is both a minister and a mother. She is the resilient mother of four adult children, and a newly elevated Elder-Elect at New Nation Church. Her leaders are Pastors Chris and Felicia Dexter. Stable and rooted in the faith, Elder Kenna renders loyal, honest, and caring service to the Body of Christ at her local church and in her spheres of influence. Kenna's life verse is Ezekiel 3:17, which says, "Son of man, I have made you a watchman for the people of Israel; so hear the word I speak and give them warning from me" (NIV).

Olympia Jarboe

OlympiYah *Ambassador for Jesus* was born Olympia Nyonomuan Jarboe. She is a first-generation Liberian-American and native of Harlem, NY. She decided to follow Jesus Christ as a teenager and later rededicated her life in her mid-20s. OlympiYah primarily works in youth ministry at her local church, and has done so for the past six years. A lover of travel and culture, OlympiYah has been on missions trips to Haiti and Cuba, and has visited several other countries. She particularly looks forward to her visits to Liberia, West Africa—the land of her heritage. Her desire is to establish a Christian educational ministry in Liberia, as she was troubled by the amount of children she saw on the streets during school hours. She has purposed in her heart to invest in the development of the youth and community.

OlympiYah currently works as a Mental Health Consultant, reviewing child welfare cases with abuse and neglect, domestic violence, as well as educational and developmental concerns. She holds a Master of Social Work with a concentration in Student-Community Development in Higher Education, a Master of Arts in International Education, a Bachelor of Arts with a concentration in Community Mental Health, a Behavioral Health-Criminal Justice certificate, and a doctoral coursework in Christian educational leadership. OlympiYah's testimony includes healing from cancer and deliverance from low self-esteem. Her desire is to see a generation of children, families, and individuals set free in Jesus' name. Two of her favorite scriptures include: Matthew 11:12, "The kingdom of heaven suffereth violence, and the violent take it by force;" and Proverbs 31:8-9 (NIV), "Speak up for those who cannot speak for themselves, for the rights of all who are destitute. Speak up and judge fairly; defend the rights of the poor and needy."

Shevon L. Sampson

Shevon L. Sampson is an author, entrepreneur and businesswomen who believes that serving the community and finding success in business go hand-in-hand. Her life-long passion for serving others led her to write her first book, "The Heart of a Sower". She has also developed a companion game board that teach money management from a biblical perspective. In addition to this fun for all board game and self-help workbook she has created a devotional. She hopes to help and inspire others with this collection, designed to get people thinking about not only their finances, but how the decisions they make about what they keep and what they give can impact their future and the futures of others.

Sampson is chief executive officer of Sowers Reap International. Sowers Reap International is the distributor of her works, including "The God Bank", "2 SOW OR NOT 2 SOW" Board Game, "The Heart of a Sower" workbook, and "Kingdom Keys for Seed Sowers" devotional.

Sampson received her Bachelor of Science in Business Management at Grand Canyon University in Phoenix, Arizona. After many years as a successful business leader, she returned to school and will be completing her Master Degree in Business Management Fall 2018.

Jackie Betty

Jacqueline Wade Betty wore the mantle of justice long before she realized it. As a young girl growing up in Jamaica, she was very vocal in her views of unfair treatment of others and often defended them. It mattered little to her that she sometimes suffered. What mattered is that her intervention got positive results. Her heart for justice is real, and she demonstrates this in her work. The judicial link between her call to champion the cause for justice and her love for accounting merged in an unusual way. A successful Charted Accountant of England and Wales who practiced in a Third World country soon learned that moving to the First World was extremely challenging. Though she quickly gained the equivalent Certified Public Accountant (CPA) license and could practice accounting, the opportunity never materialized. Thank God, she quickly learned that she could choose to take these disenfranchising punches as blows or as challenges. These punches activated another part of her purpose- writing. Her 9 years' tutoring experience in an English and Literature environment at a state college drove her to explore historical works of inequality and justice in systems.

As a CPA, she is skilled to administer financial accounting laws. Now, her skills are channeled to matters that weigh heavily on equality and justice. Among other work of poetry and music is her webpage, www.kingdomjusticealliance.com. She writes to bring awareness to her readers and invites them to purposefully unite and balance the scale of justice.

Roseline Keni

Roseline Keni is originally from Cameroon, Central Africa. Growing up, as a child, she was always passionately in love with the Lord and had a strong sense and fear for Him and His presence. By God's special grace, she possesses a Bachelor's in Sciences in Healthcare Management and a Master's in Health Sciences concentrated on Public Health. She has been married for 16 years to Evans Keni, and are both blessed with four children. Roseline and her husband are the founders and senior pastors of the Kingdom Gospel Ministries located in Reynoldsburg, Ohio.

Apart from ministering in her home church, Roseline has recently stepped out on Facebook by the leadership of the Holy Spirit in deliverance, prophecy, dream interpretation, and teaching through two ministries she just founded: Equipping Sword Ministries and Cutting Edge Women Ministries.

Niles Bess

Prophet Niles Bess has been in ministry for over 20 years preaching, teaching, activating, imparting and prophesying. With a strong apostolic and prophetic grace, Niles has helped ministries across the country establish and building effective worship ministries and leadership teams.

Niles has been uniquely anointed to minister a style of praise and worship that destroys the bondage of the enemy and brings the atmosphere of heaven. In addition to producing and song writing, Niles has authored a book entitled "Minstrels and Psalmist: The Key to Davidic Praise and Worship". This book helps to reveal the purpose and intent of the Minstrel and Psalmist in the earth.

Niles has been married to Gina Bess for over 21 years and has 3 sons. With a mandate to teach and train believers in the area of leadership and worship. He is committed to writing books as well as demonstrating and imparting the spirit worship and developing leaders around the world.

Noreen Henry

Noreen N. Henry was born in London, England and migrated to the United States in her late teens. Noreen is the Founder and CEO of Victorious Living Culture LLC, and an author; her book "Victorious Living: Guide to a Happier Life" is a #1 International Bestseller and #1 on the Hot New Releases list. She has obtained an AAS degree, an Administrative Assistant certificate, a diploma, and six certificates from Rhema Correspondence Bible School; certificates of Taking Care of People God's Way, Christian Counseling 2.0, and Eating Disorders from Lighthouse University. She has attended The Healing School; and has various other certificates. Noreen is currently pursuing a ministry degree. She is an ordained minister through Joan Hunter Ministries, and is a life-long learner that continues to study the Word of God daily. Noreen is an avid reader, and spiritual mum to many. She is a member of AACC, 4CA, KBA's Inner Circle, and the John Maxwell Team. Noreen is passionate about the things of God due to her life experiences and cares a great deal about people and our society. Noreen has gone through a lot of major challenges in her life that have made her into the person that she is today, and she plans to make the world a better place, being a legacy-changer as well as a world-changer. The song "People Help the People" was dedicated to Noreen by one of her nieces. Noreen resides in New York City and has three children and two grandchildren at the moment.

James Pinto

James Pinto is a Venezuelan-American recording artist, songwriter and musician. He has recorded 2 albums at Gaither Studios titled "Between 2 Worlds" and "Holy, Humble, and Obedient". His productions are comprised of all original songs accompanied by band, backup singers, choir and the Indianapolis Symphony Orchestra. In November 2017, James will release his new single titled "Arise & Shine" produced by the 2 time Emmy award winner Julio Castellanos who now resides in Madrid, Spain. James resides in Texas with his beautiful wife Jennifer Thomas Pinto and his 2 miniature dachshunds Landon and Deedee. He holds a Bachelor of Arts in Spanish from Florida International University, a Master degree in Pastoral Counseling from Ashland Theological Seminary and a Doctoral degree of Music Ministry in Arts & Entertainment from Primus University of Theology.

Booking Information: jamespintosings@yahoo.com, www.jamespintoministries.net

Cynthia Williams-Bey

Warrior, Trail blazer and Perseverance are just a few words that describes the most intricate parts of Cynthia Williams-Bey. Though her journey began in the violent streets of Bed-Stuy Brooklyn her road has landed her in Richmond Virginia. As 1 of 19 children, most may believe she was raised in a happy home consisting of 2 parents. The ugly truth is that she was the bi-product of her father's infidelity and her very environment would just be the nesting place for her journey down the road of heartache, betrayal, confusion and abuse. As a Wife, Mother of 5, Ambassador, Author, Visionary and International Leader, her struggles and lack of perfection is the very thing that qualifies her to uplift, encourage and free those that are walking down the same roads that kept her bound.

Cynthia is the founder of Heaven Sent Child Care which has served families in the Richmond community since 2005 with childcare until 12 midnight. She's the Serving Change Director and a Intercessor at Liberation Church, and has done missionary work in Honduras. In 2016 she was awarded Author of the Year for ACHI Magazine and in 2017 she received the "Serving Change Award" for her dedication and commitment to bring change to her community.

Adrienne J. Sumler

A New Orleans native, an Apostolic Admiral and a worshipper after God's own heart that's Apostle Adrienne J. Sumler. Over 25 years of ministry and 18 years as the founder & Senior Leader of Kingdom Ambassadorial Worship Center International; an apostolic hub center. When she is not ministering to the flock she can be found in intercession or bringing God's people through deliverance. As an apostle to the nation's, a spiritual mother to many, a natural mother to four and a wife to Claude Sumler Sr. She is blessed to call Apostle Axel Sippach her spiritual Father and is a member of the EPIC Family. If this is your first time hearing of Apostle Sumler for the first time, it certainly won't be your last!

Yolanda R. Mosby

Yolanda R. Mosby is an author, prayer intercessor, speaker and entrepreneur who stands firm on the word of God. As a minister of education, she is very passionate about teaching others about God's word. She has received an Associates Degree in Christian Theology in 2015. Yolanda resides in the Florida with 5 wonderful children.

Dr. Yolanda Powell

Dr. Yolanda Powell is a 2nd generation Apostle with a prolific call to Marketplace Ministry. She serves as a founding Board Member & Tier-1 Leader of the EPIC Global Network (Extraordinary People Influencing Culture) with Apostle Axel Sippach and has a unique mantle to scale the 7-Mountains and train others to do the same. This cutting edge trainer and master communicator is also an international speaker, author and mentor who serves as President & CEO of her own communications company, Yolanda Powell Transcontinental, LLC. Her premiere training and coaching programs are designed for Kingdom leaders, Marketplace ministers, Global gatekeepers and Corporate executives - across seven continents - on how to develop their Life Message & Signature Talk as a living trust to creatively showcase Christ in the public square and advance His Kingdom around the globe. Dr. Powell has been in ministry for nearly four decades and is also the visionary & senior leader of Dominion International Ministries, "an embassy of training and development for Kings & Priests," located just outside Washington, DC. To learn more, visit her website at www.yolandapowell.com.

Christen Cline

Christen Cline is the third eldest of eight siblings, a mother, a teacher, small business owner, an author, active in ministry, and soon to be the wife of Pastor Joseph Owusu Duah. With a background in education, she has been teaching for 16 years. Christen was ordained as God's Apostle in 2015, and later licensed in 2017. She is the overseeing minister of the Whole Woman Ministry at The Genesis Church, in Gastonia, NC. Very adamant about the things of the Lord, Christen can always be found helping others and serving the people of God.

Anita Etta

Anita has emerged as one of the most prominent and widely recognized voices in the Cameroonian American Gospel music scene today. She is known and respected for her uncompromising and unapologetic style of ministry through her songs, her writings, her live messages and her Prophetic prayer, deliverance and counseling ministry. Anita holds an MBA in Human Resources and has a successful career in corporate America. She is a dynamic business-woman and CEO of Atina Grace Corporation, a health food company doing business as Vitality Bowls Colleyville. She is Founder of Atina Music Foundation Inc., a charitable organization that spreads the gospel of Jesus Christ through various musical events, mentoring, music scholarships and donations to aspiring gospel artists. Her philanthropic activities have also included working with orphans in Africa, an incubator donation project for hospitals in her home country Cameroon, and serving on the boards of various non-profit organizations. Anita is a wife and mother of two.

Michelle Jackson

Elder Michelle Jackson is a proud member of the All Nations Evangelistic Church of Harrisburg, Pennsylvania. She serves as an ordained elder under Apostles Melvin Thompson III. She's a gifted soldier with a prophetic and apostolic anointing. Michelle Has been grace by God to do spiritual warfare and intercede for the nations. Jackson has devoted her life to serving God at the front lines of the spiritual war for people's souls. She wants others to understand how demons can enter and corrupt from within. Michelle has taught believers that stumble in their spiritual walk due to the relentless temptation of sin that they can be more than conquers. Michelle stands on God's word that true and lasting deliverance is possible when a person surrenders themselves to God. Michelle gives the right tools for total freedom and deliverance.

Jackson is also the author of Morgan Where Are You Running? To, Do You Know Your Demon? and I Decree & Declare for the Apostolic & Kingdom Minded. All books are available through Amazon.com.

Anita McCoy

Anita McCoy, with over 30 years of ministerial leadership, is a dynamic woman that God has raised up to advance His Kingdom. In 2009 Anita started "The Healing Clinic", a transformation center with an emphasis on apostolic teaching, strategic prayer, prophecy and the ministry of healing. In addition to this, as Founding Pastor and Director of Field of Dreams Harvest Ministries (2013), Anita has a mandate to raise leaders through apostolic and prophetic training, and discipleship. She has ministered in various parts of the United States, as well as East Africa and India. Anita also serves the Northwestern region of Pennsylvania as Vice President of Leadership Development of Aglow International, an international Christian organization of women and men comprised of over 200, 000 members ministering in 171 nations worldwide. Anita, a graduate of Bloomsburg University of PA, received her Bachelors of Science in Education with a minor in Speech and Audiology and credits her love of education and revealing truth as key components that fuel her passion to reproduce reproducers who are equipped and empowered to fulfill their God-ordained destiny and influence all cultures of society through the dynamics of Heaven's Kingdom Culture.

www.ingramcontent.com/pod-product-compliance
Lightning Source LLC
Chambersburg PA
CBHW080400170426
43193CB00016B/2769